THE MEANING (

THE MEANING OF THEISM

Edited by
John Cottingham

Blackwell
Publishing

© 2007 by Blackwell Publishing Ltd

First published as Volume 19, No. 4 of *Ratio.*

BLACKWELL PUBLISHING
350 Main Street, Malden, MA 02148-5020, USA
9600 Garsington Road, Oxford OX4 2DQ, UK
550 Swanston Street, Carlton, Victoria 3053, Australia

First published 2007 by Blackwell Publishing Ltd

Library of Congress Cataloging-in-Publication Data has been applied for

ISBN-13: 978-1-4051-5960-9

A catalogue record for this title is available from the British Library.

Set in 11pt New Baskerville
by SNP Best-set Typesetter Ltd., Hong Kong
Printed and bound in the United Kingdon
by TJ International, Padstow, Cornwall

The publisher's policy is to use permanent paper from mills that operate
a sustainable forestry policy, and which has been manufactured from pulp
processed using acid-free and elementary chlorine-free practices.
Furthermore, the publisher ensures that the text paper and cover board
used have met acceptable environmental accreditation standards.

For further information on
Blackwell Publishing, visit our website:
www.blackwellpublishing.com

CONTENTS

List of Contributors   vii
Preface   ix

1 What's God Got To Do With It? Atheism and
   Religious Practice   1
   David Benatar

2 What Difference Does It Make? The Nature and
   Significance of Theistic Belief   19
   John Cottingham

3 Philosophy, the Restless Heart and the Meaning
   of Theism   39
   John Haldane

4 Worshipping an Unknown God   59
   Anthony Kenny

5 'Seeke True Religion. Oh, Where?'   71
   Michael McGhee

6 The Varieties of Non-Religious Experience   91
   Richard Norman

7 Divine Action in the World (Synopsis)   111
   Alvin Plantinga

Index   121

CONTRIBUTORS

David Benatar
Philosophy Department
University of Cape Town
Rondebosch, South Africa

John Cottingham
Department of Philosophy
The University of Reading
Reading, UK

John Haldane
Department of Moral Philosophy
University of St Andrews
Fife, UK

Anthony Kenny
St John's College
Oxford, UK

Michael McGhee
University of Liverpool
Department of Philosophy
Liverpool, UK

Richard Norman
University of Kent
Canterbury, UK

Alvin Plantinga
Department of Philosophy
University of Notre Dame
Notre Dame, IN, USA

PREFACE

The Meaning of Theism is the latest volume to appear in the RATIO
special issues series, which has now been running for twelve years.
The first volume, *Truth in Ethics*, edited by Brad Hooker, was
published in 1995, and since then the series has attracted
enormous interest, covering a wide range of topics of central
importance in contemporary philosophy, ranging from metaphysics and ethics to philosophy of science, philosophy of mind, and
the theory of meaning.

The series has grown out of the one-day conferences held at
the end of the Easter vacation each year at the University of
Reading, under the auspices of its Philosophy Department, where
the journal RATIO is edited. The papers delivered at the
conferences, with additional articles from invited contributors,
are published in the December issue of RATIO in the year following the conference, and then appear in book form a few months
later. Each of the previous volumes has been edited by one of
my Associate Editors at Reading, to whom I am grateful for or-
ganizing a hugely successful series of conferences and for editing
the subsequent volumes. Seldom can a journal editor have
been fortunate enough to benefit from the support of such an
outstandingly able and hard-working team of associates.

The principle of Buggins's turn has, however, finally caught
up with me, and it fell to me to organize the RATIO conference
on 'The Meaning of Theism', held at Reading in April 2005,
out of which the present volume has grown. The speakers at the
conference were Anthony Kenny, John Haldane, Richard
Norman and Alvin Plantinga, and additional contributions were
subsequently provided by David Benatar, Michael McGhee and
myself.

Much philosophical work in the philosophy of religion, albeit
of excellent quality, has operated on a somewhat abstract plane,
as if the issues involved were (as the telling phrase has it) of

'academic' interest, rather than matters of deep importance in the lives of those involved. For that reason, I was keen that the contributors to the present volume should write with an eye to what belief in God, or its absence, *means* for the subject—what difference it makes to the flow and perceived significance of someone's life. The book's title reflects this emphasis: instead of one of the classic debates in philosophy of religion, on the arguments for God's existence, for example, or divine foreknowledge and free will, or the problem of evil, the reader will find that the various writers tackle the question of religious belief, or its absence, more from the standpoint of their own individual commitments and outlooks on life. The contributors have been chosen to represent a number of different perspectives—Christian, Jewish, Buddhist, atheist and agnostic, with a view to offering the reader a fruitful and stimulating juxtaposition of views.

The articles are arranged in alphabetical order of author. Each author has provided an abstract at the start of his paper, so I shall not provide further summaries here, but will merely offer a brief overview. In the first paper, David Benatar, referring to the importance of orthopraxy within the Jewish tradition, discusses the value and significance of religious observance irrespective of belief. My own contribution, which also raises questions about the supposed centrality of belief in religious allegiance, discusses the role of emotions and habits of virtue in the adoption of a religious outlook. The next paper, by John Haldane, representing a mainstream Catholic position, focuses principally on the human desire for God, and its significance as supporting traditional religious belief. There then follows Sir Anthony Kenny's contribution, in which he develops the idea of 'devout agnosticism', that is to say a position that advocates the value of religious worship despite serious doubts about whether humans can know anything about the existence or nature of God. Michael McGhee, whose paper includes several references to traditions of Buddhist spirituality, explores the relation between theological commitments and religious 'sensibility', explained in terms of the underlying spiritual and moral conditions in which belief or its absence emerges. In the penultimate paper, Richard Norman, writing from a humanist perspective, discusses various kinds of so-called religious experience, and argues that these can be given an interpretation that is consistent with naturalism or atheism. Finally, the celebrated philosopher of religion Alvin Plantinga addresses the relationship between religion and science, arguing, in the face of the widespread conviction that they are in tension, that they can be shown to be entirely compatible. I am grateful to the distinguished authors included here for their contributions to a topic of enduring importance. There were periods during the latter half of the twentieth century when it sometimes seemed as if issues about God and religion might become marginalized within the mainstream philosophical academy. That now seems out of the question: philosophy of religion and philosophical theology are vigorously alive, and there appears to be a keen and growing interest in these subjects among students and general readers alike. Few issues could be as momentous as the question of whether one is to adopt a religious or a naturalist worldview, for that choice colours so much of our conceptual landscape, moral, scientific, and personal, infusing almost every aspect of how we live. It is my hope that this collection will throw some light on some of the ways in which that choice is being addressed in our contemporary intellectual culture.

John Cottingham
Editor, RATIO.
Reading, January 2007.

1

WHAT'S GOD GOT TO DO WITH IT? ATHEISM AND RELIGIOUS PRACTICE

David Benatar

Introduction

An old Jewish joke tells of the young questioner who wanted to be apprenticed to the great *apikoros*[1] (heretic) of Minsk. He makes the journey to Minsk and meets the great man, but is soon disappointed. He notices that the *apikoros* keeps his head covered, is punctilious about the dietary laws, observance of the Sabbath and the rest of the Torah. No longer able to contain himself, he asks the older man: 'How did you get the reputation of being such a great *apikoros* when I see that you observe all the commandments?' 'Ah, an *apikoros* I am', replied the master, 'but a *goy* (gentile) I am not'[2].

In insisting that there is nothing incongruous about a heretic's practising traditional Judaism, the punch line itself sounds incongruous. It is my aim to show that there is indeed nothing incongruous in this insistence – that there is nothing incoherent about a heretic, even of atheistic proportions, practising traditional Judaism. Although the notion of the 'orthodox heretic' *is* incoherent (where the term is not an ironic criticism of unreflective heresy), the idea of the 'heretical practitioner of Judaism' is not. Among those who recognise that it is not incoherent, many will think that it is nonetheless odd. Why, it will be asked, would a non-believer practise a religion? I shall answer that question too. I focus on Judaism primarily because, for reasons I shall outline

---

[1] The etymology of this Hebrew (and derivatively Yiddish) word for heretic is 'Epicurean'.

[2] A colleague of mine, Jeremy Wanderer, used a version of this joke at the beginning of his paper 'The Future of Jewish Practice' in Nicholas de Lange & Miri Freud-Kandel, eds., *Modern Judaism: An Oxford Guide* (Oxford: Oxford University Press, 2005), pp. 254–264. As I told him the joke and suggested that he use it there, my use of it here should not be construed as plagiarism. It should go without saying, however, that I am obviously not the source of the joke. As with so many jokes, the source is unknown (to me) and thus, regrettably, cannot be acknowledged.

later, it lends itself to the possibility of separating belief and practice. There may well be other religions of which this is also true, but I do not have the same familiarity with them. Heresy obviously can take many forms. The greater the number of beliefs, the greater the number of ways to be heretical. Similarly, the more rigid the orthodoxy the more mild a deviation is thought (by the orthodox) to count as heresy. My concern here is not simply with any deviation from orthodoxy or even with simply any form of unbelief. I shall focus on what is arguably the most basic of religious beliefs, belief in God, the rejection of which is commonly thought to have bearing on religious observance. And I shall focus on a particular kind of rejection of this belief – not agnosticism, but rather atheism. I focus on this more difficult case, noting that what I say applies *a fortiori* to agnosticism.

The common view and its errors

It is commonly thought that belief in God, coupled with a belief in the divine authorship of the Bible (or other sacred text) entails orthopraxy – adherence to the full range of normative religious practice. One observes because this is what God's timeless commandments require one to do. The corollary, it is thought, is that atheism entails something quite different. Many people assume that it entails the opposite – namely complete abandonment of all (non-moral) religious practices. Not all have this view, however. At least since the Enlightenment and the emergence (during the *Haskala*, or Jewish Enlightenment) of non-Orthodox[3] versions of Judaism, very many Jews have seen alternatives to comprehensive religious observance, namely a more selective observance, that they maintain in spite of their atheism or other departure from Jewish orthodoxy.[4] In other words, atheism is commonly thought to entail one of two conclusions – either no religious observance or a reformed religious observance.[5] Those who assume the first

[3] I use 'Orthodox' with a capital 'O' to denote the Jewish denomination and 'orthodox' with the small 'o' to denote traditional doxastic conformity. Part of what I shall be arguing in this paper is that orthodoxy does not entail Orthodoxy.
[4] Not all non-Orthodox Jews are atheists, which is why I also refer here to *other* departures from Jewish orthodoxy.
[5] The dominant non-Orthodox denominations in Judaism are Reform Judaism (sometimes called 'Progressive Judaism', by its adherents, of course) and Conservative Judaism (with a capital 'C'). The latter, which gets its name relative to Reform not Orthodox

entailment will be puzzled even by the suggestion that reformed religious practice is an alternative entailment. Much of what I shall say about atheists who adhere to full traditional practice, will apply also to those non-believers who reform or selectively adopt religious practice. In this way, I shall make both the atheistic reformer of religious practice and the atheistic adherent of orthopraxy intelligible to those who assume that atheism entails the abandonment of all religious practice. However, it is because religious reform is so common a response to atheism, at least within Judaism, that I present it here as part of the common view about what atheism entails for religious practice.

I reject all of the foregoing claims about entailment. Belief in God and the divine origin of a sacred text, contrary to the common view, need not entail orthopraxy. Nor need atheism entail either the abandonment of all religious practice or reformed religious practice. This is not to deny that orthopraxy is a reasonable response to the belief in God and the divine origin of the Bible. Nor is it to deny that abandoning religious practice entirely, or changing it, are reasonable responses to atheism. My claim is only that theists and atheists are not committed to these outcomes. There are alternatives.

Orthodox heteropraxy

Although the atheist is my main concern in this paper, it is worth considering the theist first, showing why he[6] is not committed, in virtue of his theism, to orthopraxy. For reasons that will become clear later, this also has relevance for the case of the atheist.

There are obvious cases of theists adopting different religious practices – namely theists of different religions. Christians, for example, although they believe in God and accept the Hebrew Bible as being God's word, do not observe all the ritual laws of what they call the 'Old Testament'. This is because, in addition to their belief in the divine origin of the Hebrew Bible, they also hold other beliefs – most particularly a belief in a second revelation, of the 'New Testament', which they take to supersede the earlier

---

Judaism, occupies the middle ground between the two. I shall use the adjective 'reform' (with a small 'r') to refer generically to those denominations that are not 'Orthodox' (with a capital 'O').

[6]　For a justification on the use of the male pronoun see my 'Sexist Language: Alternatives to the Alternatives', *Public Affairs Quarterly*, 19(1) (2005), pp. 1–9.

one. Although the most obvious, this is not the most interesting way, as far as my argument is concerned, in which theists can vary in their religious practices. This is because for all the common theological ground between Judaism and Christianity, there is also much theological difference. Jewish orthodoxy and Christian orthodoxy are quite different and it might be thought that each of these entails a different orthopraxy. I need to show, therefore, how Jews who subscribe to Judaism's beliefs could logically avoid Jewish orthopraxy.

They could do so by reforming what they take to be divinely given law. Although many Orthodox Jews deny that Jewish law has changed, this view is manifestly false. There are many practices that were once permitted but now are not – including polygamy and divorcing a wife without her consent.[7] Whereas these are all cases of the law's becoming more stringent – what is biblically permitted becomes rabbinically prohibited – there are also cases where the biblical law (arguably) became more *lenient* as a result of rabbinic emendations. For instance, the sage Hillel noticed that the biblical provision that debts be cancelled in the sabbatical year was leading to people not making loans to the poor in advance of the sabbatical year because they feared that the loans would not be repaid. Because this imposed further burdens on the poor who were unable to obtain much needed loans, Hillel instituted a legal mechanism whereby the loan could be transferred to the court and collected after the sabbatical year.[8] The letter of biblical law was subverted via a technicality in order to preserve the spirit of the law – benefiting the poor.

It is a point of some contention whether the Talmudic rabbis acknowledged how different rabbinic practice was from the practice of biblical Judaism. It is unlikely that they were all of one view. There is evidence, however, that (at least) an influential strand of Talmudic thought did indeed recognise the innovative role of the rabbis and thus the difference between Jewish practice in the Talmudic and biblical eras. Some go further and claim that this strand of Talmudic thought is the dominant one.[9] Whether or not

---

[7]   These two practices were prohibited by an enactment of Rabbi Gershom in approximately 1000 CE. It only applied to Ashkenazi Jewry, but today's Sephardi Jews do not diverge from Ashkenazic practice in this matter.
[8]   Mishna, *Gittin* 4:3.
[9]   This is the view of Menachem Fisch, *Rational Rabbis: Science and Talmudic Culture* (Bloomington: Indiana University Press, 1997). According to him, those he calls the

this stronger claim is true, it is sufficient for my purposes to show that there is an influential strand of rabbinic thought that sees Jewish practice as fluid and evolving rather than static.

One piece of evidence for this view is an interesting item of rabbinic lore. According to this story,[10] when Moses ascended to heaven to receive the Torah, he noticed that God was adding small 'crowns'[11] to the letters. When he asked as to the purpose of those crowns, God disclosed that many centuries in the future, a sage, Rabbi Akiva, would deduce many laws from these crowns.[12] Moses wanted to see this scholar and God transported him forward in time to the academy of Rabbi Akiva. Moses, the Talmud relates, was unable to follow the discussion and felt despondent. Then, one of the students asked Rabbi Akiva from where he had derived his teaching. Rabbi Akiva responded that it had been handed down from Moses to whom it had been given at Sinai. At this point, we are told, Moses became comforted.

In this story, we hear the stunning acknowledgement that the Torah taught by Rabbi Akiva and which, according to traditional Jewish belief, was handed down from Moses, would not be understandable to Moses himself. The most plausible explanation of this, it seems to me and to many others, is that the Torah had undergone a process of legal development over the intervening generations.

This rabbinic view of the difference between the law believed to be given by God and the law of the rabbis is further illustrated by another, arguably more brazen story. The Talmud gives an account[13] of a debate between Rabbi Eliezer and the rest of the sages regarding a question of ritual purity that was moot at the time of discussion (because the Temple was no longer standing). So confident was Rabbi Eliezer of his position that he kept invoking miracles to bear testimony to the correctness of his view. According to the Talmudic story, each of these miracles occurred, but the rabbis were not swayed. Eventually a heavenly voice called out testifying that Rabbi Eliezer was indeed correct. Unimpressed by even this, Rabbi Joshua rose to his feet and declared of the

---

'antitraditionalists' prevailed over the 'traditionalists'. The former, on his view, saw the halachic process as innovative and not merely a transmission from earlier generations.

[10]   Babylonian Talmud, Tractate *Menachot*, 29b.
[11]   Some Hebrew letters in Torah scrolls are written with 'crowns' on top.
[12]   This is but a metaphor. There are numerous ways in which laws are derived, but derivation from crowns on letters is not among them.
[13]   Babylonian Talmud, Tractate *Baba Metzia*, 59b.

Torah, 'It is not in heaven!'[14] – that although it was given at Sinai, heavenly voices have no place in its interpretation, decisions regarding which must be made by the majority of sages.

We see then that even on a – possibly *the* – Talmudic view, Jewish law *does* change. Assuming this, what really differentiates today's Jewish denominations, contrary to the common view about this matter,[15] is not a difference of view about God's existence or about the divine origin of the Torah.[16] Instead, what differentiates them are differing views about how (much) the law may be changed. What characterises Orthodox Judaism is not orthodoxy, as its name suggests, but rather a more conservative view of the acceptable limits of change. Reform Judaism by contrast is characterised by an embracing of radical change. It is quite possible for somebody to believe that the Torah is the word of God and yet to subject it to greater change, perhaps because he holds the view that word of God has to be reinterpreted for each age. Whether that change is true to the earlier principles of change or rather a rupture in the Jewish legal tradition is another matter that I shall not pursue here. All we need recognise is that one can reform a scripture that one believes is authored by God.

Now it may be argued that although theists could reform a law that they believe to have been given by God, they depart from Jewish orthodoxy in another way – namely in their belief about the acceptable mechanisms, principles or limits of legal change or innovation. However, to make this move is to stipulate so broad a definition of 'orthodoxy' that any heteropraxy ceases, by definition, to be orthodox. This definitional move does not engage the relevant sense of orthodoxy that is central to my argument. I am arguing that orthodoxy in the sense of belief in God does not entail orthopraxy. That claim is not affected by noting that there may be some other sense of orthodoxy that *does* entail orthopraxy.

In any event, the broader definition of 'orthodoxy' is unfortunate if one accepts, as many Talmudic rabbis did, the distinction

[14] Here Rabbi Joshua was quoting Deuteronomy 30:12.
[15] One advocate of the common view is Mordecai Kaplan. In speaking about how Orthodoxy differs from non-orthodox denominations, he says that '[o]rthodoxy assumes that religion must be based upon the authentically attested supernatural revelation.' *Judaism as a Civilization* (New York: Schocken Books, 1967), p. 313.
[16] Many people in both the Orthodox and non-Orthodox denominations accept that what differentiates them are different views about the origin of the Torah. Thus, my claim is not one about what Orthodox and non-Orthodox Jews say motivates them. Instead, my claim is about what I take to be the best way of conceiving of the difference.

between heresy – denial of a core principle (an *ikkar*) – and the legal disagreement that pervades rabbinic Judaism. The Talmud, for example, is filled with disagreements between the rabbis about what the law requires. Of such disagreements it is said 'both these and these are the words of the living God'.[17] In other words, conflicting legal interpretations, by accepted rabbinic authorities, both have legitimacy. Although Orthodox Jews would deny that heteropraxic interpretations are legitimate, this does not mean that they are unorthodox (even if they are un-Orthodox).[18]

Heterodox orthopraxy

Just as theists are not logically committed to orthopraxy, so atheists are not logically committed either to the reform or to the abandonment of all (non-moral)[19] religious practice. Atheists can engage, without contradiction, in orthopraxy. For example, an atheist might view the origin of the religious practice as unimportant. It simply might not matter to a particular atheist whether the practice is of divine origin or a human invention.

To appreciate this point about the origin of a religion's practices, we might consider an analogy with a (non-religious) legal system. Imagine, for example, that it were discovered that some country's ancient Constitution had not been adopted under the circumstances previously thought. Perhaps it becomes evident that it was not developed at a constitutional assembly of founding fathers and adopted as a whole, but had rather developed piecemeal over decades or centuries. Would that commit citizens to cease obeying the laws? Would it require the rejection of that country's long history of constitutional law? Would the precedent of constitutional interpretation be voided? A negative answer to these questions is not implausible. It just may not matter whether the mythology of the Constitution's origin is true or not. All that might matter is that the country has a long and stable legal tradition that has great value to its citizens.

Religious practices similarly can be valuable, even to some atheists. Put another way, there can be non-theistic reasons for observing religious practices. Engaging in religious practices might, for

---

[17] Tractate Eruvin 13b & Tractate Gittin 6b.
[18] See note 3 above.
[19] I add this condition because those religious practices that have a moral basis are often thought to have value independent of theism.

example,[20] have sentimental value, provide a sense of tradition, or be thought either to add another valuable dimension to family life or to be good for the children. Alternatively, or in addition, religious practice can be both an expression of and a means of fostering an (ethnic) identity. I shall focus on identity as a non-theistic basis for religious practice. I do so not because the other reasons must be subsumed under it – although for many people they are. Instead, I focus on identity because it seems to me to be the most oft-cited non-theistic reason for religious practice. I shall treat it as an exemplar of such reasons rather than as the sole such reason. Much, but not all, of what I shall say about identity also applies to the other reasons.

Many Jews take Jewish practice to be essential to the long-term preservation of the Jewish people. On this (not implausible) view, although individual Jews can continue to be Jews without practising Judaism, the Jewish people cannot survive across generations in the absence of religious observance (by at least some Jews). Those who believe this and who place value on Jewish continuity may engage in Jewish practice in the absence of religious belief.[21]

---

[20] I have heard all the non-theistic reasons I shall now mention from heterodox orthopractic Jews.

[21] Bryan Magee refers to this basis for heterodox Jewish observance. As an aside, it should be added that he has some odd things to say about Jewish orthodoxy:

> Of the religions that I have studied, the one I found least worthy of intellectual respect was Judaism. I have no desire to offend any of my readers, but the truth is that while reading foundational Jewish texts I constantly found myself thinking: 'How can anyone possibly believe this?' When I put that question to Jewish friends they often said that no intelligent Jew did. To quote the precise words of one: 'There's not a single intelligent Jew in the country who believes the religion'. What they do believe, they tell me, is that it is desirable that traditional observances should be kept by at least some Jews because it is these observances more than anything else that give the Jewish people its identity and therefore cohesion, but the doctrinal content or implications of the observances are not expected to be taken with full intellectual seriousness by intelligent people.
> [Bryan Magee, *Confessions of a Philosopher* (London: Weidenfeld & Nicolson, 1997) p. 368.]

There are a number of questions that come to mind while reading this passage. First, what are these foundational Jewish texts that he is reading? The Hebrew Bible? That is a poor guide to Jewish doctrine. The Talmud? But the Talmud is not a book of doctrine. Neither, for that matter, is the *Shulchan Aruch* (the Code of Jewish Law). Indeed, I do not know of any foundational Jewish text that provides some standard of Jewish doctrine. (There are a few non-foundational ones, but their views are contested within Judaism.) Second, although I share Professor Magee's response to Jewish doctrines – 'How can anybody possibly believe this?' – I cannot understand why he should think that Jewish doctrines are

The claim that religious observance can be founded on considerations of identity will sound odd to those whose notion of religion has nothing to do with ethnicity. However, if they consider those religions that are also markers of ethnicity, atheistic observance of religious practices for ethnic reasons should not be very surprising. Judaism is one such religion. It is the religion of an ethnic group – the Jews. I shall say more about this later, but for now I note only that there are very many Jews who, although they do not believe either in God or the divine origin of the Torah, nonetheless engage in some observances.

Observance, of course, is a matter of degree. Among those atheistic Jews who do observe at least some religious practices, the degree of observance ranges from very little to everything. Some only circumcise their sons (for reasons of identifying as Jews). Some also fast on the Day of Atonement or hold a special celebratory Passover meal. Others observe much more than this.

It is obviously a minority of atheist Jews who observe all, or almost all, Jewish religious practices. They are a minority for two related reasons. First, the full set of observances is obviously more onerous than a subset. Although there is no logical bar to full observance for an atheist, there can be psychological difficulties. Keeping up that level of observance in the absence of religious belief may be difficult for many (but not all). Second, most Jewish atheists for whom Jewish identity is important feel that observing a more limited set of Jewish practices is sufficient to satisfy their sense of identity. They thus derive the benefits of identity-motivated religious observance without having to bear the costs that they would bear if their religious observance were more extensive. However, some Jewish atheists are neither satisfied with the lesser observance nor burdened by the greater observance, and thus there are some who, in their practice, are indistinguishable from practising orthodox Jews. Just as atheism is not incompatible with minimalist observance, so it is also not incompatible with maximalist observance.

---

harder to believe than those of other religions. Indeed, Jewish doctrine is economical relative to the other Abrahamic faiths. That is to say, Christianity and Islam accept the core beliefs of Judaism and then add some – the virgin birth, the divinity of Jesus, or the status of Mohamed as the supreme prophet. I would have thought that, at least to the sceptical mind, adding these beliefs to those of Judaism only makes the doctrinal soup of Christianity and Islam harder to swallow.

When is a religion more conducive to atheistic observance?

I have shown, so far, that the link between theism and religious practice can be much weaker than it is often thought to be. Estrangement, and even divorce, of the two, is possible. Whether or not this is true of all religions, it is certainly true of a religion such as Judaism. I turn now to consider those features of Judaism that facilitate the possibility of atheistic orthopraxy.

Ethnic religion

The first of these features, to which I have already referred in passing, is the ethnic nature of Judaism. Judaism is the religion of an ethnic group – the Jews – and the Jews are an ethnic group that is defined in some way by a religion – Judaism.[22] Judaism does not purport to be a universal religion – a religion for everybody. It does not view itself as the sole means to 'salvation', and thus does not proselytise[23] – indeed it usually actively discourages prospective converts. Instead Judaism views itself as an ethnic-specific, or, in earlier parlance, a tribal religion. This explains why Judaism does not impose a doxastic condition for inclusion in the Jewish people. A Jew, according to Judaism, is not somebody who holds certain beliefs – or even a person who performs certain practices. Instead a Jew is somebody born of a Jewish mother[24] – or somebody who converts to Judaism. Even in the case of converts, acceptance of beliefs is not technically required, although acceptance of the commandments is required.[25] Most Jews, however, are Jews by birth. If they never come to hold any of the beliefs associated with Judaism, they do not cease to be Jews, according to Judaism. Moreover, they might want, despite their heterodoxy, to identify

---

[22] Some go so far as to deny that Judaism is indeed a religion (in the usual sense, at least). One alternative is that it is a civilisation. See M. Kaplan, *Judaism as a Civilization.*

[23] This is not true of all of Jewish history. There were periods when some proselytism did take place and there are even rare instances of forced conversions (such as the Idumeans, from whom Herod was descended). However, these are aberrations from the norm.

[24] In contrast to the principle of matrilineal descent, characteristic of most of Jewish history, Biblical Judaism accepted patrilineal descent. In our times, Reform Judaism does not restrict itself to (either patrilineal or) matrilineal descent.

[25] A convert's failure to observe after conversion, however, does not invalidate the conversion retroactively.

as Jews. The most obvious ways of doing that are via Jewish religious practices.[26]

The priority of practice over belief

The second feature of Judaism that enhances the possibility of atheistic orthopraxy is the priority that Judaism gives to practice over belief. Although a Jew who neither believes nor practices does not cease to be a Jew, all Jews are nonetheless obligated, according to Judaism, to act in accordance with Jewish precepts. Although there is some disagreement within Judaism about whether Jews are also required to believe certain things, the overwhelmingly dominant view is that they are not.[27] More specifically, belief, on most views, is not among the precepts that have to be obeyed.[28] Thus, according to Judaism, Jews are required to do some things and refrain from doing others, but they are not obligated to believe anything. This is not to deny that belief is viewed widely within Judaism as being important. It is only to say that on most views belief is neither an obligation nor as important as practice.

This is conducive to the Jewish atheist who wishes to identify as a Jew via Jewish practice. Judaism's lesser emphasis on what one believes means that one is not, in the ordinary course of religious life, called upon to state one's beliefs.[29] There is rather little interest in what one believes and much more interest in what one

[26] In our time, two dominant alternative routes to self-identifying as a Jew are via Holocaust remembrance and Zionism. Each of these, however, has its difficulties. Many Jews are critical of expressing one's identity only by responding to anti-semitism. Zionism may not do as good a job of bypassing Judaism as some of its secular adherents would like. Can Jews be identified in any enduring way in the absence of Judaism?

[27] See, for example, Menachem Kellner, *Dogma in Medieval Jewish Thought* (Oxford: Oxford University Press, 1986).

[28] In my 'Against Commanding to Believe', *Shofar: An Interdisciplinary Journal of Jewish Studies*, 19(2) (2001), pp. 87–104, I argue, on philosophical grounds, against a commandment to believe. I then show how this conclusion is compatible with traditional Jewish thinking (or at least influential strands of such thinking).

[29] Judaism's view towards practising Jewish atheists bears some resemblance to the US military's policy regarding gays in its midst – a 'don't ask, don't tell' policy. The only difference is that, in Judaism, if you *do* tell about your atheism, you do not cease to be Jewish (although it was once possible – and may still be possible in very closed ultra-orthodox communities – to be excommunicated).

does. Judaism does include, of course, direct and indirect statements of faith. They occur, most obviously, in prayer. However,
given that the fixed prayers are standardized for the entire community and are required even of those who do not believe, the
mere utterances of the statements cannot and are not assumed to
be individual declarations of faith.

Legalistic religion

A third reason why Judaism enhances the possibility of atheistic
orthopraxy is that it is a legalistic religion. This feature connects
with the previous one. Law is a better regulator of practice than it
is of belief. Thus the legalistic nature of Judaism partly explains its
greater emphasis on practice than on belief. But the influence can
work in the other direction too. A religion with greater emphasis
on practice lends itself to legalism more than one that is primarily
concerned with belief.

When I say that Judaism is a legalistic religion I do not mean
merely that it has a legal system. I mean also that law plays a much
greater role than does theology or any other area of religious
thought. In Judaism the paradigmatic scholar is not the theolo-
gian and certainly not the mystic, but rather the Talmudist and
halachist – or scholar of *halacha*, Jewish law. Moreover, as we saw
earlier, law acquires a life of its own in Judaism, at least on the view
I am defending. When Rabbi Joshua overrides a heavenly voice
and asserts that the Torah (Law) is not in heaven, he asserts if not
its primacy, then certainly its independence from its origin. We
have here a kind of separation of powers. If legislation is believed
to have taken place at Sinai, then ongoing judicial interpretation
is the domain of the rabbis (Jewish legal scholars) and not God.
The rabbis did not give the Torah and God does not interpret it.

We can see immediately how a religion characterized by this
kind of legalism is, at least to the extent that any religion could be,
relatively friendly to atheists. If religion is more about law than
about God – or even if it merely can be viewed that way – then
atheistic religious observance is a real possibility. Consider again
the analogy I provided earlier of the ancient Constitution that is
discovered not to have originated in the way that it had previously
been thought to have arisen. Insofar as the subsequent tradition
of law has taken on a life of its own, its legitimacy is not dependent
on its origin. Similarly, Judaism's mythology about the origin of

the Torah may be irrelevant, in the eyes of those motivated by other considerations, to the ongoing value of law.[30]

Considering objections to heterodox orthopraxy

I have argued that heterodox orthopraxy is a coherent possibility. There may well be those who nonetheless will view it with suspicion. I turn now to consider their concerns. Although the responses are implicit in the arguments I have already advanced, I shall render them explicit here.

Inauthenticity

The first objection is that there is something inauthentic or dishonest about an atheist observing religious practices. To perform religious practices without accepting religious beliefs is not authentic *religious* practice. Religious practice, on this view, must have its source in religious belief. Religious practice in the absence of belief is mendacious – it falsely suggests that the practitioner has certain beliefs.

Now the problem with this objection is that it presupposes the very view of the relationship between belief and practice that I have rejected. That is, it assumes that religious practice makes no sense in the absence of belief. That assumption, however, is insufficient to rebut an argument to the contrary. Those who think that religious observance makes no sense in the absence of religious

---

[30]   Although Yeshayahu Leibowitz would reject the explicitly pragmatic foundation for religious observance just mentioned, he shares the view that the mythology about the origin of the Torah is irrelevant to Jewish religious praxis. He declares that his 'approach to the subject of the Mitzvoth [commandments], and to Jewish religious praxis . . . is not that of history or theology'. ['Religious Praxis: The Meaning of Halakhah' in Yeshayahu Leibowitz, *Judaism, Human Values and the Jewish State*, Eliezer Goldman, ed. (Cambridge MA: Harvard University Press, 1992), p. 3. His concern is not historical but contemporary. Of Jewish law he says that '[c]ontroversy and diversity of opinion abound within its framework, yet the opposed views are all regarded as 'the word of the living God'' [Ibid.] 'What characterizes Judaism as a religion of Mitzvoth', he says, 'is not the set of laws and commandments that was given out at the start, but rather the recognition of a system of precepts as binding, even if their specifics were often determined only with time' [Ibid., pp. 3–4.] See also Avi Sagi, 'Yeshayahu Leibowitz – A Breakthrough in Jewish Philosophy: Religion Without Metaphysics', *Religious Studies*, 33(2), pp. 203–216. Nevertheless, it is unclear whether Professor Leibowitz is a theist or an atheist. He is (often obstinately) vague about this. See Joshua O. Haberman, *The God I Believe In* (New York: The Free Press, 1992), pp. 127–152.

belief would have to say why they think that is so. At the very least they would need to undermine my argument that some atheists could have non-theistic reasons for religious observance. A claim of inauthenticity is not sufficient, because if I am correct there can be more than one authentic basis for religious observance. Moreover, if there can be non-theistic reasons for religious observance, then the atheist's religious practice does not mendaciously imply that he is a theist.

The foregoing is not to deny there seems to be something odd about atheists offering prayers and doing 'God-talk'. But this is only so if one takes prayer literally to be communication with God. Matters are different if one views it more metaphorically or merely as another ritual. Those atheists distanced from religious practice might not see any value in such rituals, but that does not mean that those atheists close to the religious practices must follow suit. I might wonder how you (or anybody) could love your spouse, but that does not matter. What matters is that *you* love her. Nor need I take literally the sweet nothings that you mutter to her. You call her 'pumpkin' or 'baby'. You do not mean that she is these things; nor need I take you to be saying that she is. Your uttering these words in this context is intended to and does function differently from somebody's uttering the same words in a different context – such as while pointing at a pumpkin or a baby. Something similar may be said about atheists talking about and 'to' God. The word 'God' in their mouths is (in some respects) like the word 'pumpkin' in yours.

Atheistic practitioners might note that they would much rather that their ethnic identity were not so intricately bound up with religious practices including, most significantly, prayer. However, given that their ethnic identity *is* bound up with such practices and is important to them, performing these practices and uttering these ancestral formulations is valuable. It may not have the same kind of significance that it has for theists, but that does not mean that it lacks significance of another kind.

Religious practice requires appropriate intention

A second and related objection is that a practice cannot be a (true) religious practice unless it is motivated in the right kind of way – unless, that it, it is done with the right intention. Atheists, according to this objection, lack the requisite intention and thus

although they may be going through certain motions that
resemble religious observance, they cannot be said to be engaging
in religious practices.

One can stipulate that religious practice requires theistic intentions or beliefs, in which case the objection holds. However, the
interesting question is whether one *must* accept the view that
religious practice requires theistic intentions. In support of such a
requirement, at least within Judaism, it might be noted that there
is a Talmudic principle that *mitzvot tzrichot kavana* – (the performance of) commandments requires (appropriate) intention.[31]
However, this is a principle in dispute. Even if the principle is
accepted, there are various possible readings of what kind of
intention it requires. We can distinguish at least three kinds of
intention, only one of which is sufficiently strong to support the
objection. The first kind of intention is what we might call 'mere
intention' – the intention to perform the required action (or to
refrain from performing a prohibited action). Requiring mere
intention invalidates unintentional, or accidental performance of
a religious practice. The second kind of intention is what we might
call '*mitzva*-intention' – which is the intention to perform the
action because it is a *mitzva* (commandment or precept). Finally,
there is what we might designate as 'God-intention' – the intention to perform the practice because it is an obligation *from God*.[32]
I have shown elsewhere that, with one possible exception, the
principle need not be understood as requiring anything more
than *mitzva*-intention.[33] The one possible exception is the obligation to read the *sh'ma*.[34] However, because requiring God-
intention raises some logical problems, as I show, it would be
preferable if, in all cases, the principle of *mitzvot tzrichot kavana*
were interpreted to require no more than *mitzva*-intention. If that
is so, then we can reject the view that a practice is a religious
practice only if it is motivated by theism. Even if this cannot be
extended to the *mitzva* of reading the *sh'ma*, Judaism would still
require atheists to read the *sh'ma* without God-intention. In other
words, even if theistic belief is essential for the complete fulfil-

---

[31] See Tractate *Berachot* 13a–13b and Tractate *Rosh Hashana* 28a–28b.
[32] Contrary to what some might think, there *is* a difference between the second and
third kinds of intention. See my 'Against Commanding to Believe', p. 101.
[33] 'Against Commanding to Believe', pp. 98–104.
[34] Deuteronomy 6: 4–9.

ment of that *mitzva*, its absence is not sufficient to exempt anybody
from the *mitzva.*

Explanations and imperatives

A third objection is that whereas some atheists want to and do
observe religious practices, there is no reason why they *must* do
so. Theists by contrast, it might be argued, have reason for
thinking that they are obligated to observe. In other words, we
can only offer a psychological explanation of an atheist's religious practice, but we cannot say why the atheist *must* observe
the practices that he does observe. By analogy, we can offer a
psychological explanation of why somebody who, as a child, was
bitten by a dog now fears dogs, but this explanation does not tell
us that the person has a reason for thinking that he *should* fear
dogs. Psychological explanations are not imperatives. They have
no normative force.

In response, I readily acknowledge that there are some atheists
who engage in religious practice and who have no reason for
thinking that they should do so. They do so merely for conve-
nience, or on a whim, for example. By the same token, however,
there are also theists who, for the reasons I outlined earlier, have
no reason for thinking that they must perform particular religious
practices. (Theism, I argued earlier, does not entail orthopraxy.)
And just as there are other theists who do have reasons for thinking that religious practice is something they must do, so there
are some atheists who have reasons for thinking that they must
perform religious practices. Theistic and atheistic imperatives for
religious practice have different sources. For atheists, unlike
theists, God is not the source of the imperative. Instead, the
source is some commitment coupled with a (non-religious) belief
that religious practice is essential to that commitment. Thus an
atheist might be committed to his ethnic identity and take religious practice to be essential to (the preservation of) that identity.

Precariousness

I turn finally to a fourth and related concern. The worry here is
that religious practice grounded on some atheistic imperative is
more precarious than religious practice grounded in theism.
Absent either the underlying commitment or the belief that religious practice is essential to that commitment, the atheist has no

grounds for taking religious practice to be obligatory. The atheist's religious practice is precarious because its foundation could evaporate.

There are two possible interpretations of this concern. Under one interpretation, the claim is that atheistic religious practice is *logically* more precarious than theistic religious practice. On this interpretation, the objection fails. This is because we can make a parallel claim about theistic religious practice: Absent religious belief, the theist who observes (merely) for theistic reasons has no grounds for taking religious practice to be obligatory. In other words, remove the belief and this erstwhile theist – now an atheist – has no reason to continue practising.

An alternative reading of the concern has it that atheistic religious practice is *psychologically* more precarious than theistic religious practice. The idea here is that it is psychologically easier for an atheist to drift away from religious practice than it is for a theist to do so.[35] This is obviously an empirical claim and thus cannot be answered *a priori*. If the claim is false then the second reading of the precariousness objection also fails. But what if the claim is true? It is still not clear what the objection is meant to achieve. The objection must come from those who value religious practice, for otherwise there could be no concern about the precariousness of religious practice. However, if that is the case, then we might ask what difference it makes whether religious practice that is grounded in atheism is more precarious. An atheist has no *other* foundation for religious practice. The theistic foundation has already failed him. It is either this or nothing.[36]

Conclusion

I have argued that although there are strong psychological connections between theism and religious practice, and between

---

[35] I assume that the objection does not have in mind those atheists who never engage in religious practice – because we cannot speak of their religious practice being precariously grounded. It is probably true that most religious practitioners – and certainly the overwhelming majority of orthopractic ones – are theists. Thus I'm happy to grant that theism is psychologically a greater inducement to religious practice than are any of the atheistic grounds.

[36] Some theists might recommend a programme of indoctrination, but there are serious questions about the ethics of belief that arise here. For more on this, see my 'Against Commanding to Believe'.

atheism and the absence of religious practice, theism does not entail religious practice and atheism does not entail its abandonment. I showed how a theist could have reasons to depart from orthopraxy and how an atheist could have reasons to observe religious practices, either minimally or maximally. It does not follow from this that the answer to the question posed in the title of this paper – What's God got to do with it? – is always 'nothing'. For those theists who perform religious practices only because of their theism and those atheists who do not practice but would do so were they theists, God has everything to do with their practice or non-practice. For others, however, theism or its denial makes no difference to religious practice. This is true of the theist who does not practice and of the atheist who does. It is also true, however, of those theists who have both theistic and non-theistic reasons (of decisive weight) for religious practice. Their commitment to religious practice is over-determined. Although they happen to believe, it would make no difference, so far as their religious practice is concerned, if they did not.[37]

[37] I am grateful to Jeremy Wanderer and David Goldenberg, who share my interest in this topic, for their helpful comments, as well as to an anonymous reviewer for *Ratio*.

WHAT DIFFERENCE DOES IT MAKE? THE NATURE AND SIGNIFICANCE OF THEISTIC BELIEF[1]

John Cottingham

1. Theism and doxastic freight

What difference does theistic belief make to the believer? It is often assumed, particularly by philosophers, that the main difference is a cognitive or doxastic one: that the theist has a radically different belief-map of the world from the atheist or the agnostic. A comment I once heard addressed to a recent convert illustrates this: 'I imagine your view of things is very different now that God is in the picture.'

Yet this cannot be quite right: for if we leave aside deities like those of the Greek pantheon, living atop Mount Olympus, most theists don't think of God as being 'in the picture', in the sense of inhabiting the world; indeed, on the standard conception put forward by Aquinas and others, God is not an individual being at all, not an 'entity' alongside the other entities in the world, but is rather the source of all being.[2] So it is not as if the theist's inventory of the universe includes some extra item that is absent from the atheist's list.

But even if the theist's and the atheist's lists of objects and events comprising the natural world may be the same, perhaps the two inventories might differ in respect of *supernatural* entities? On

---

[1] Earlier versions of this paper were delivered during 2005–6 at the Butler Society, Oxford University, at the D Society, Cambridge University, and at a University of Reading colloquium on the philosophy of religion held at Salisbury. I am grateful for comments received by the participants at these events, and especially to Douglas Hedley, Joseph Jedwab, Brian Feltham, Severin Schroeder, Bart Streumer and David Oderberg. I am also grateful to Thad Metz and to Sam Vice for comments.

[2] God exists 'outside the realm of entities, as a cause that pours forth every entity in all its variant forms' (*extra ordinem entium existens, velut causa quaedam profundens totum ens et omnes eius differentias*). *Commentary on Aristotle's* Peri Hermeneias [*Sententiae super Peri Hermeneias*, 1270–71], I, 14. Quoted in B. Davies, *Aquinas* (London: Continuum, 2002), p. 74. The divine simplicity, as Davies also explains, precludes talk of God as an individual (*Aquinas*, Ch. 7).

this view, sceptics or agnostics doubt the existence of such entities; hard-nosed atheist naturalists flatly deny it, regarding the domain of the supernatural as empty – or perhaps, on the hardest-nosed version of all, even denying that it makes sense to speak of such a domain; but theists, plonking down the existential quantifier, assert that, apart from the natural world, there exists an x such that . . . x is omnipotent, the creator of all, and so on. (And indeed they may go on to assert that several other supernatural things exist – angels, for example, or souls.) Such assertions, quantifying over a domain wholly other than the totality of natural objects and events, have traditionally been called 'metaphysical'. Theists, then, so runs the suggestion, are distinguished from atheists by their possession of a certain class of metaphysical beliefs. I say 'a certain class', because not all metaphysical claims are theistic or supernaturalist: there is a flourishing branch of contemporary 'metaphysical' philosophy that investigates notions such as substance, time, change, identity, and so on, which may (at least on some views) be instantiated only in the ordinary natural world. We might perhaps usefully distinguish 'heavy' metaphysics, transcendent, supernaturalist metaphysics, from this other more modest academic brand, which could (without any disrespect)[3] be called 'metaphysics lite'.

People often assume, then, that 'heavy' metaphysical commitments are crucial in distinguishing the theistic from the atheistic or agnostic standpoint.[4] But to set against this common assumption[5] it is worth noting that there is actually not a vast number of metaphysical claims in many of the most central religious texts,

[3]   The disclaimer is important, since in terms of the sophistication and depth of its arguments, there is nothing whatever lightweight about contemporary academic metaphysics; the 'weightiness' I am referring to by making this distinction is purely a matter of whether supernaturalist and transcendent claims are involved.

[4]   An important exception to the standard linkage between theism and metaphysics is the recent 'postmetaphysical theology' typified by the work of Jean-Luc Marion (which, however, approaches these issues from a very different angle). See Marion's *Dieu sans l'être* [1991] transl. by T. Carlson as *God without Being* (Chicago: University of Chicago Press, 1991), and the excellent essay by Carlson, 'Postmetaphysical theology' in K. Vanhoozer (ed.), *The Cambridge Companion to Postmodern Theology* (Cambridge: Cambridge University Press, 2003).

[5]   It is interesting that such an assumption is often so ingrained as to be retained irrespective of what is actually asserted by defenders of a theistic position. To cite but one small example, a recent otherwise highly acute and discerning discussion of my *On the Meaning of Life* managed in one respect to misconstrue the argument, by automatically assuming that it must be resting the possibility of a meaningful human life on the existence of an immortal soul – whereas in fact a commitment to afterlives and souls is not invoked

including for example the Bible. This may be a familiar point to theologians, but philosophers, especially those who prefer to attack from a distance, often assume the contrary. To mention just one instance, the view of human life found in much of the Bible far from supports the common conception of the religious outlook as regarding our ordinary natural existence as merely a pale preparation for some future state. Much of the Hebrew Bible (the Psalms are a prime example) is remarkable for the overriding value it seems to accord to *this* life. The same goes for quite a bit of the New Testament. Thus Jesus rebuffs attempts to draw him on the issue of the resurrection of the dead, and in answer to the question of who would be the post-mortem husband of the widow who had married seven times, he replies that marriage is not something that applies to such a future state;[6] at the very least this rejects any idea of the after-life that construes it as a kind of ameliorated prolongation of what we have enjoyed on earth. Speaking generally, it seems a radical misconception to think of Christianity as holding that we don't need to worry about present ills because everything will be reversed afterwards.[7] In this context, the story of Jesus' reaction to the death of Lazarus is surely significant: he most emphatically didn't say 'Don't worry, it's all going to be fine!'; on the contrary, according to the shortest verse in the Bible, he wept.[8] The whole of Christ's reported ministry makes it clear that enormous weight is placed on the need to alleviate human suffering, illness and premature death, and that responding to such need and pain is most certainly not something that becomes less urgent in virtue of belief in a future existence.

But whatever the case regarding souls and the afterlife, it might seem that there is one distinctive and indispensable piece of cognitive metaphysical freight that distinguishes the theist from the atheist, namely the belief that God exists. That such a belief

anywhere in the book. See Thaddeus Metz, 'Cottingham and Baier on the Meaning of Life', *Disputatio*, Vol. I, no. 19 (December 2005), pp. 215–228. Cf. J. Cottingham, *On the Meaning of Life* (London: Routledge, 2003).

[6] Matthew 22: 23–33. In the course of his answer, Jesus asserts 'God is not the God of the dead, but of the living' (v. 32).

[7] There is a story of the late Cardinal Basil Hume phoning various friends when he discovered he had cancer, and after receiving many sympathetic reactions of the form 'Oh I'm so sorry', getting from one fellow-Christian a joyful cry 'Oh congratulations!' The idea presumably was to express a flattering confidence in the Cardinal's fitness for a heavenly reward, but the quoted comment seems a ghastly parody of the proper Christian response to illness and death.

[8] John 11:35.

does distinguish the theist from his opposite is something I do not
want to dispute (though it's perhaps worth noting parenthetically
that there are those who without obvious absurdity claim to be
religious adherents without being theists in this sense).[9] But I want
in this paper to maintain that the theist's willingness, if such it be,
to assert the truth of this proposition, existentially quantifying
over a supernatural domain, is actually not a very helpful way of
marking out the difference between the theist's and the atheist's
world views.

2. Outlooks, emotions and frameworks

To approach the possibility of an alternative way of characterising
the theistic outlook, it will be helpful to go back to the work of one
of the logical positivists of the mid twentieth century. This group
of thinkers is often thought to have bluntly dismissed all religious
language as meaningless, but a number of them took a consider-
ably less sweeping and more nuanced position. Among these was
Rudolph Carnap, who observed that if sentences about God were
merely collections of nonsensically juxtaposed words, they could
hardly have occupied so many 'eminent minds' in 'all ages and
nations'. The assertions of religious believers did have a meaning,
allowed Carnap, but he went on to say that it was a mistake to
construe them as referring to states of affairs. They serve instead,
Carnap suggested, for the expression of the general feeling or
attitude of a person towards life (*Lebensgefühl*); and he went on to
make a comparison between religious talk and poetry:

> The metaphysician believes that he travels in territory in which
> truth and falsehood are at stake. In reality, however, he has
> not asserted anything, but only *expressed something, like an artist*
> ... [T]he metaphysician [mistakenly aims to support] his state-
> ments by arguments, he claims assent to their content, he
> polemicizes against metaphysicians of divergent persuasion by
> attempting to refute their assertions in his treatise. Lyrical
> poets, on the other hand, do not try to refute in their poem the

9   See David Benatar, 'What's God got to do with it?' (present volume); see also D.
Cupitt, *Taking Leave of God* [1980], 2nd edn. (London: SCM, 2001).

statements in a poem by some other lyrical poet; for they know they are in the domain of art and not in the domain of theory.[10]

The idea that religious language is analogous to poetry has a certain appeal; indeed much of it – canticles, psalms, hymns and so on – *is* poetry. And something useful, I believe, can be salvaged from Carnap's notion of religious assertions as expressing a certain outlook on life. To be usable, however, what might be called Carnap's *expressivism* needs pretty drastic modification.

First, the implied contrast between expressing something and making truth-claims seems suspect. Even poets, after all, aim to disclose truths about the world and the human condition; indeed one might well think that the truths they disclose are often particularly striking and important (albeit – or perhaps partly because – they are not simply prosaic records of 'the facts'). Second, and connectedly, there also seems to be something confused about Carnap's suggestion that religious (and for that matter poetic) language serves to express a *Lebensgefühl*, a *feeling* or *attitude* towards life, if 'attitude' is here being construed as something radically distinct from the domain of statements and propositional contents. It is not as if a feeling or attitude towards some object is simply some kind of inarticulate, non-statable, non-propositional cry of rage, or grief, or joy, or exaltation. If, for example, I write a piece expressing my attitude to the war in Iraq, then it seems very implausible to say that on the one hand I produce statements that describe factual states of affairs, and on the other hand I supplement it with a few grunts or moans. Recent work on the emotions has begun to correct this kind of simplistic and polarised picture. Michael Stocker has argued that emotional states such as anger and pity can have a vital role in directing and focusing our attention, thus radically affecting the way we perceive things: 'they seek out and collect, even create, sustaining or concordant facts . . . which they then use to justify and sustain that emotion, which then leads to further seeking, collecting, creating and coloring.'[11] The emotions, as Mark Wynn has nicely put it, have

---

[10]   Rudolf Carnap, 'The elimination of metaphysics through logical analysis of language' [*Überwindung der Metaphysik durch Logische Analyse der Sprache*, 1932]. First published in *Erkenntnis*, vol. II. Trans. Arthur Pap, in A. J. Ayer (ed.), *Logical Positivism* (New York: Free Press, 1959), p. 79 (emphasis supplied).

[11]   Michael Stocker with Elizabeth Hegeman, *Valuing Emotions* (Cambridge: Cambridge University Press, 1996), p. 94. Cited in Mark Wynn, 'The relationship of religion and ethics:

a role in 'guiding enquiry by constituting patterns of salience.'[12] An evaluation of an event, or an expression of one's attitude, is thus often an inextricable mix of the cognitive and the emotive; or perhaps we should say instead that much of our attitudinal language is inherently resistant to the implied separation between 'pure' cognitive content and an emotional 'add-on'.[13]

The upshot is that if I have a certain attitude towards an event such as the war in Iraq, an attitude of hope, for example, or of despair, that stance should certainly not be construed as a 'feeling' [*Gefühl*] that is isolated from the rest of my cognitive network of beliefs. It would be better to say that my outlook depends on an intricately interlinked pattern of intellectual and affective responses that together comprise what might be called a *framework of interpretation*. So something may perhaps after all be salvaged from Carnap, if we say (bearing in mind the various the caveats about 'expression' and 'attitude' just noted) that the user of religious language is often not so much referring to different facts or states of affairs from those referred to by the atheist, but instead is using it to express a certain outlook or attitude to the same facts. With this in mind, I want to take some I hope relatively uncontroversial examples of distinctively religious attitudes, to examine how a religious framework of interpretation affects the way the believer perceives the world.

3. Humility and hope

If we are looking for types of attitude that are distinctive of a religious outlook, it makes sense to start with the classic Christian virtue of humility. From a purely naturalist perspective, it might well be supposed that this is not a virtue at all. It is significant, for example, that it holds no place in Aristotle's schema of the virtues. There is, for Aristotle, the virtue of having a due sense of how much lavishness and external grandeur one's station in life demands – *megaloprepeia*, or magnificence; and this virtue is

---

A comparison of Newman and contemporary philosophy of religion', *Heythrop Journal*, 2005. See also M. Wynn, *Emotional Experience and Religious Understanding: Integrating Perception Conception, and Feeling* (Cambridge: Cambridge University Press, 2005).

[12]   Mark Wynn, 'The relationship of religion and ethics'.

[13]   See J. Cottingham *The Spiritual Dimension* (Cambridge: Cambridge University Press, 2005), Ch. 5.

flanked by a corresponding vice of excess – vulgarity or crude self-display, and a vice of deficiency – mean-mindedness or pettiness (*microprepeia*). But humility as such, putting oneself last, as enjoined in various Gospel parables, is simply absent from this particular Greek pattern of commendable or deplorable dispositions and attitudes. Moving to a slightly different dimension of the worthwhile life, Aristotle goes on to speak of a distinctive virtue of *proper ambition*, a justified desire to secure the honour that is one's due. This is contrasted with its vice of excess, the tendency (as we might say) to be over-pushy, and on the other hand with its vice of deficiency, an insufficient zeal for honour and fame; but here again there is no way of fitting genuine humility into the schema. Finally, in the sphere of what one says and thinks, as opposed to what one does, Aristotle acknowledges the virtue of *proper self-estimation*, of telling the truth about oneself; this has a vice of excess, boastfulness, but at the other end of the scale we do not have humility, but instead a vice of deficiency called *eironeia*, which is a tiresome disposition to conceal or understate one's due merits; again, humility simply doesn't fit anywhere in this particular scale.[14]

The secular naturalist has a dilemma here, I think. Either she can go along with Aristotle and simply accept a schema of proper human character and conduct that allows no place for humility; or she can acknowledge the moral pull of something like the Christian conception of humility and try to find a secular analogue for it. What exactly is humility then, in the Christian framework of interpretation? Firstly, it is a certain forbearance, a readiness, as in the parable, not to stride up to the place of honour, but to take a lower seat, and wait until one may be asked to 'go up higher'.[15] This implies, perhaps, a consciousness of one's own defects, but it also implies a certain purity of character – an inner integrity, a lack of anxious concern to insist on matters of status, a recognition that one is but one among many others, and that one's gifts, if such they be, are not ultimately of one's own making. Religious language offers a ready expression for this complex framework of affective and cognitive responses. Man is not self-creating: 'It is he who hath made us and not we ourselves'. The mighty may 'boast and trust in the abundance of their riches',

---

[14] For these various virtues and vices, see Aristotle, *Nicomachean Ethics* [c. 325 B.C.], Bk. IV, esp. Chs 2, 4, 7. For the general triadic scheme of the virtues, each with a flanking vice of excess and of deficiency, see Bk. II, Ch. 8.

[15] The parable of the wedding guest: Luke 14:10.

but the righteous man, though 'poor and needy' is 'like a green olive tree in the house of God, trusting in the mercy of God for ever.'[16] The quotations could be multiplied endlessly; and the framework they imply is one in which humility has a recognized and stable place. Remove the framework, and the injunction to be humble can start to look arbitrary and unsupported. For an exhortation to virtue is not just a raw set of prescriptions on how to act, or on what dispositions to cultivate; it necessarily involves a *background of significance,* a wider picture of the goals of human life, or the best way of living. Without such a background picture, any given candidate for a virtue or vice will be isolated from its source of meaning; to change the metaphor, it will be like a plant that grew in a certain soil, which could theoretically be uprooted and transported to a different climate and conditions, but which in reality cannot properly take root and thrive there.

The above quotations referring to humility also serve to introduce another distinctively religious cluster of virtues, those of faith, hope and trust. 'O Israel, *trust* in the Lord', says the Psalmist, 'for in him there is mercy, and in him is plenteous redemption.' Or again, 'I *hope* for the Lord; my soul doth *wait* for him; in his word is my *trust.*'[17] Again, there is no proper placeholder for these traits in Classical virtue theory; on the contrary, one of the characteristic features of ancient Greek thought, both in Aristotle and in the tradition he inherited, was a distinctly sober, not to say gloomy, awareness of how often hopes can be disappointed, of how easily human life can be overturned, even for the most virtuous and prosperous, by the swings of fortune.[18] 'Call no man happy until he is dead', ran the proverb, etched deep into the mindset of most of the philosophers and poets of classical antiquity.[19] But the cry of Job, 'Though he slay me, yet will I trust in him',[20] or St Paul's 'neither height nor depth nor . . . things present nor things to come . . . shall be able to separate us from

[16] For these various quotations, see Psalms 100[99]:3; 49[48]:6; 40[39]:17; 70[69]:5; 52[51]:8. Translation and numbering of chapters from the King James version and/or the Book of Common Prayer (the alternative numbering in square brackets is that of the Vulgate and Septuagint versions).

[17] Psalm 130[129]:5–7.

[18] See Aristotle on the terrible misfortunes suffered by King Priam at the end of what had hitherto been a prosperous and happy life: *Nicomachean Ethics,* Bk I, Ch. 10.

[19] The saying is attributed to the ancient lawgiver Solon, but is found, for example, at the end of Sophocles' play *Oedipus Tyrannus* (mid 5th century BC).

[20] Job 1:4.

the love of God',[21] express something quite outside the range of this Classical fatalism: an indomitable determination to trust and to keep hope alive, to 'hope against hope', as Paul put it in his Letter to the Romans.[22]

Again, I suggest, the naturalist faces a dilemma here. On the one hand, it is hard to deny that there is something admirable about this ethic of hope and trust. And the value is something we seem to recognize not just on a prudential level (though there may be some evidence that people stranded in a lifeboat who can keep their hopes up are more likely to survive for longer than those who despair). Over and above such utilitarian considerations, most of us have a strong intuitive sense of something splendid, something moving, about the human being weighed down with misfortunes and difficulties, who nevertheless manages to keep alive the radiance of hope, as is done in the straining yet resonant self-exhortation at the end of the forty-third Psalm: 'Why are thou cast down, O my soul, and why are thou disquieted within me? Hope in God for I shall yet praise him who is the health of my countenance, and my God.'[23]

The position so far reached, then, is that these so-called theological virtues are ones which many or most of us, almost irrespective of religious persuasion or its absence, can intuitively recognize as admirable and valuable. And hence, short of biting the bullet and suppressing such intuitions, the naturalist has to construct some secular analogue for these virtues, which will allow them to be preserved as ethically desirable traits of character. But I have suggested that this will not be easy, without a suitable framework in which to locate them. A recent valiant attempt to translate them into a purely secular context has been made by Erik Wielenberg, in his study *Value and Virtue in a Godless Universe*. In the secularized schema offered by Wielenberg, humility becomes a recognition of 'the tremendous contribution *dumb luck* has made to all human accomplishments', so that 'taking the balance of credit for one's accomplishments is foolish'.[24] The central theological virtue of hope, maintained in the face of radical vulnerability and the ever-present human tendency to

---

[21] Romans 8:38.
[22] Romans 4:18.
[23] Psalm 42 in the Vulgate.
[24] E. J. Wielenberg, *Value and Virtue in a Godless Universe* (Cambridge: Cambridge University Press, 2005), pp. 110, 112.

buckle under external misfortune or internal weakness, becomes a confidence in the power of science to ameliorate our lot (including by pharmacological means), pointing us towards 'the upper limits of justice and happiness' that 'remain to be discovered'.[25]

What is interesting about these Wielenbergian virtues – recognition of our dependence on fortune, and optimism about the progress of science – is what one might call the 'thinness' of their psychological profile. A judicious assessment of how far one's advantages are due to genetic and environmental contingencies; a carefully argued (but presumably revisable) positive estimate of what can be achieved by scientific advance: these seem more like positions for debate than deeply ingrained dispositions of emotion and action. Without going into whether or not they are worthy beliefs to cultivate, they are not integrated, as the religious virtues are, into a complex psychological story about self-discovery, moral growth through suffering, and what the spiritual writers called *metanoia* (changed awareness). What Wielenberg has given us, it seems to me, are essentially 'static' doxastic features of a rational secular outlook; there may be nothing wrong with this, but what is left out, in the process of constructing the secular analogues, is almost every motivational and psychological aspect of the spiritual life that has made the traditional religious virtues intelligible and attractive to those who aspire to them.

Let us now bring all this to bear on our central question of what distinguishes the theist from the atheist. I have so far suggested that a difference in doxastic metaphysical baggage is not as helpful a criterion as many philosophers often suppose for separating the outlook of the theist from that of the atheist. What has now, I hope emerged, is that the theistic outlook offers to its adherents a complex interpretative framework for human life, a framework within which certain intuitively precious virtues find a secure place. So in approaching the ancient question 'How should one live?', theists are able to draw on a rich tradition of parables and poems and hymns and prayers, which orient them towards certain goals, including the cultivation of humility and of hope, that would otherwise be difficult or impossible to fit into an intelligible ethical schema.

What this points us towards, I suggest, is a very different way of drawing the distinction between the theist and the atheist from

---

that of applying a 'thin' propositional test based on how each would answer the yes/no question 'Do you or do you not believe in a supernatural being called "God"?' It is not so much that applying this latter test will necessarily give us the wrong answer, as that it may predispose us to get the focus wrong – to assume that the key difference between theism and atheism is one of 'cold' belief or philosophical argument (as it might be in the case of, say, the difference between internalism and externalism in the theory of action), as opposed to a practical difference in the respective models for living, and how their significance is interpreted.

All this (as I shall come on to discuss in the final section) cannot entirely be just a 'practical' or pragmatic matter, but will also inevitably imply differences in the respective networks of understanding possessed by theists and atheists. But for now the point I wish to underline is that the main difference between the theist and the atheist turns out (if I may put it this way) to be hermeneutical rather than factual – a matter of the interpretative structures employed rather than the facts assented to. For example, there is not, or need not be, any major disagreement between the theist and the atheist about the principal features of the human predicament, or the observable circumstances surrounding our human existence. The theist's 'human world' is precisely the selfsame world as that which the atheist inhabits – a world of pain and loss, of vulnerability and danger, and, even in the case where the individual comes through unscathed, of eventual inevitable physical and mental deterioration and, finally, death. This tragic dimension, what Pascal called the 'wretchedness' of the human condition, is not in any way ignored or glossed over by the theist – quite the contrary: a glance at almost any of the sacred scriptures, or the classic texts which bookshops group under the 'spirituality' section, will establish the point. But what is offered is an ethical framework for interpreting that human world, a framework in which certain virtues are given special grounding and significance, and in which, as a result, there is hope that 'the good can be achieved and evil endured'.

That last phrase is in fact a quotation famous as an Epicurean motto – the motto of a philosophical system that was to all intents and purposes atheistical.[26] And in the light of this, one might well

---

[26]   *Aphobon ho theos. Anhypopton ho thanatos. To agathon eukteton. To deinon euekkartereton.* ('Nothing to fear in God. Nothing to worry about in death. Good can be attained. Evil Can

raise the question of whether a theistic outlook is indeed necessarily linked to the adoption of the kind of complex ethical framework just referred to – a framework, that is, which finds a place for such virtues as humility and hope. In an attempt to indicate a route to answering this, I will in the next section briefly discuss two further attitudes that are generally thought to be distinctively religious, namely awe and thankfulness; this done, I shall return, in the final section, to the question of metaphysical freight, which may seem still to be lurking noisily in the background despite all the focus so far on the practical domain of ethical virtues and frameworks for living.

4. Awe and thanksgiving

The starry heavens above were for Immanuel Kant a principal source of what he called 'awe' (*Achtung*).[27] A sense of wonder at the grandeur of the universe, the splendour and vastness of the night sky, is something that figures in many ancient religious writings, of which perhaps the best known is the psalm *Caeli enarrant gloriam Dei*, 'The heavens declare the glory of the Lord'.[28] Some atheists have protested sharply at the theist trying to appropriate wonder and awe as part of the religious outlook,[29] but it turns out, as we found in the case of humility and of hope, that it is not particularly easy to construct purely secular analogues of these reactive attitudes. Of course it would be foolish to deny that committed atheists can enjoy a rich and complex aesthetic appreciation of the natural world; one does not need to check someone's religious allegiance, or lack of it, to decide whether they can

be endured.') The celebrated 'four-fold remedy' (*tetrapharmakon*) is found in the first century BC Epicurean philosopher Philodemus, *Adversus sophistas*, 4 (quoted in A. A. Long and D. N. Sedley (eds), *The Hellenistic Philosophers* (Cambridge: Cambridge University Press, 1987), 25 J). The adjective *anhypopton* in the second sentence means literally 'unsuspected', or (in this context) 'nothing to be suspicious about, nothing to worry about'. An alternative version has *anaistheton* – 'nothing to feel in death' or 'death is total unconsciousness' (cf. Epicurus, Letter to Menoeceus, 124, in Long and Sedley 24A). I say that Epicureanism was 'to all intents and purposes' atheistical because there is scholarly controversy over the sense in which the School may have allowed the existence of the 'immortals' or 'gods'; but at all events they were held to be of no relevance to human life.

[27] Immanuel Kant, *Critique of Practical Reason* [*Kritik der Practischen Vernunft*, 1788], conclusion. Transl. T. K. Abbott (London: Longmans, 1873, 6th edn 1909). In *Kant's gesammelte Schriften*, Akademie edition (Berlin: Reimer/De Gruyter, 1900–), 5:161.

[28] Psalm 19[18].

[29] Cf. Richard Norman, 'The Varieties of Non-Religious Experience' (present volume).

be having a powerful experience when they look at the sunset over the ocean and say 'Wow!'. But awe implies something rather more than this.

To begin with, there is a link with humility. The contemplation of the vastness of the universe is, as Pascal noted, particularly evocative of the puniness of humankind beside the unbounded cosmic backdrop against which we play out our tiny existence.[30] But this sense of the cosmic insignificance of humankind is only part of the story. Awe implies more than a sense of fear at something vastly greater than oneself; it also suggests a recognition of the grandeur and splendour of that greater thing – what in the Hebrew Bible is called *kavod*, 'glory'. This term, hard to translate, appears in the first verse of the Psalm just referred to ('The heavens declare the *glory* of God'), and it is interesting to note that the response evoked by such perceived 'glory' is not merely an 'aesthetic' one, in the rather thin modern sense which we sometimes use when referring to the frisson someone may get from looking at a sunset or a beautiful flower; it is a recognition of that which is both magnificent and wondrous in itself, and which also calls to something in our *moral* nature. The same Psalm just cited (one which must certainly have inspired Kant's linkage of the starry heavens above and the moral law within) proceeds directly from acknowledging the the 'glory of the Lord' as manifested in the heavens to extolling the 'law (*torah*) of the Lord', which is described in terms that are no less awestruck: the law of the Lord is perfect, rejoicing the heart, enlightening the eyes, more desired than gold, sweeter than honey. These responses would be very inadequately described as 'aesthetic'; they are, rather, a complete submission of the whole mind, intellectual, sensory and moral, to something vastly greater and more perfect than itself, something

---

[30] 'I see these frightening expanses of the universe that shut me in, and I find myself stuck in one corner of this vast emptiness, without knowing why I am placed here rather than elsewhere, or why from out of the whole eternity that has gone before me and the whole eternity that will follow, this one tiny period has been given me in which to live out my life. I see only infinities on every side which shut me in like an atom, like a shadow that lasts only an instant . . .' (*Je vois ces effroyables espaces de l'univers qui m'enferment, et je me trouve attaché à un coin de cette vaste étendue, sans que je sache pourquoi je suis plutôt placé en ce lieu qu'en un autre, ni pourquoi ce peu de temps qui m'est donné à vivre m'est assigné à ce point plutôt qu'à un autre de toute l'éternité qui m'a précédé, et de toute celle qui me suit. Je ne vois que des infinités de toutes parts, qui m'enferment comme un atome, et comme une ombre qui ne dure qu'un instant.*) Blaise Pascal, *Pensées* [c. 1660], ed. L. Lafuma (Paris: Editions du Seuil, 1962), no. 427.

to which we react with humility and yet with joy, something whose
'glory' is fearful precisely because it is fearfully and wholly good.
That same remarkable fusion of aesthetic and moral and
sensory response may be found in many descriptions of encounters with what is sometimes called the 'numinous'. One such
account occurs in Kenneth Grahame's classic *The Wind in the
Willows*, an account slightly tinged with the sentimentalism characteristic of its time, but nonetheless vivid in its impact:

> On either side of them, as they glided onwards, the rich
> meadow grass seemed that morning of a freshness and a green-
> ness unsurpassable. Never had they noticed the roses so vivid,
> the willow-herb so riotous, the meadow-sweet so odorous and
> pervading . . . In midmost of the stream, a small island lay
> anchored, fringed close with willow and silver birch and
> alder . . . In silence they landed . . . And suddenly the Mole felt
> a great Awe fall upon him, an awe that turned his muscles to
> water, bowed his head, and rooted his feet to the ground. It was
> no panic terror – indeed he felt wonderfully at peace and happy
> – but it was an awe that smote and held him and without seeing
> he knew it could only mean that some august Presence was very,
> very near . . . Sudden and magnificent, the sun's broad golden
> disc showed itself over the horizon . . . and dazzled them. When
> they were able to look once more, the Vision had vanished, and
> the air was full of the carol of birds that hailed the dawn.[31]

The language has some affinities with the nature poetry of William
Wordsworth, and in particular the famous 'Lines Written above
Tintern Abbey' that may partly have inspired it:

> I have felt
> A presence that disturbs me with the sense
> Of elevated thoughts; a sense sublime
> Of something far more deeply interfused
> Whose dwelling is the light of setting suns,
> And the round ocean, and the living air
> And the blue sky, and in the mind of man . . .[32]

[31] Kenneth Grahame, *The Wind in the Willows* [1908] (London: Penguin, 1994), Ch. 7.
[32] *Lines written a few miles above Tintern Abbey* [1798], in S. Gill (ed.), *William Wordsworth: a critical edition of the major works* (Oxford: Oxford University Press, 1984), lines 89–100. For further discussion of the philosophical significance of this passage, see J. Cottingham,

To speculate about the precise metaphysical implications of the sentiments expressed here is in a certain sense beside the point. For the unmistakably religious orientation of the passage depends less on doctrinal commitments than on the characteristic way in which the poet's response fuses together elements of the aesthetic and the moral, recognizing the goodness and beauty of the cosmos in a way that intimately relates it to human concerns. The vision, once glimpsed, says Wordsworth a few lines later, gives us something that no subsequent pain or distress can entirely erase, a 'cheerful faith that all which we behold/Is full of blessings.'[33]

The notion of 'blessing' leads me to mention one final disposition or attitude characteristic of the theistic outlook, namely a readiness to see the circumstances of human life, and indeed human life itself, as *gifts* – that is, as fit to evoke responses of thankfulness and praise. This is manifested in many aspects of religious praxis – for example in stylised routines of prayer and praise performed regularly throughout each day. (Elaborated examples of this are the obligations of the Divine Office associated in the Christian tradition with specialised religious orders; but a more basic routine, for example of morning and evening prayer, is widely practised by laypeople throughout Christianity and Judaism; and as *salah*, praying to Allah five times a day, is taken in Islam to be one of the basic duties of every believer.)[34] The idea is a simple one: to put it at its most high-minded, the required mindset is that each new day be seen as a blessing, as a gift to be used to for the development of one's own talents and for the good of one's fellow human beings. A similar conception underlies the practice of saying grace at meals, as is nicely brought out by Leonard Kass in the following passage:

'"Our natural guide . . .": Conscience, "nature" and moral experience', in D. S. Oderberg and T. Chappell (eds), *Human Values; New Essays on Ethics and Natural Law* (London: Palgrave, 2005), pp. 11–31.

[33]   *Tintern Abbey*, lines 135–6 (emphasis supplied). Similarly, in the Grahame passage, the 'presence' sensed turns out to be that of a 'friend and helper', inspiring a response of 'love'.

[34]   *Salah* is the second of the 'five pillars' (*arkan ad-din*) or basic duties of Islam, the others being the *shahadah* (avowal that there is no God but Allah and Muhammad is his prophet); *zakat* (almsgiving); *sawm* (fasting in Ramadan) and *hajj* (pilgrimage to Mecca once in a lifetime). The 'avowal' requirement of course takes us beyond mere praxis – a point to which we shall return in the final section.

A blessing offered over the meal still fosters a fitting attitude toward the world, whose gracious bounty is available to us, and not because we merit it . . . The materialistic view of life, though it may help put bread on the table, cannot help us understand what it *means* to eat . . . Recovering the deeper meaning of eating could help [us] . . . see again that living in a needy body is no disgrace and that our particular upright embodiment orients us toward the beautiful, the good, the true and the holy.[35]

It is again difficult not to see something admirable about the practices and attitudes so described; and again the question of whether one should acknowledge their value puts the atheist in a similar kind of dilemma to that which I have posed earlier. To bite the bullet and deny all value to such practices seems harshly out of tune with our intuitions; but to attempt to preserve what is valuable in them while discarding the theistic vehicle in terms of which they are expressed seems doomed to failure, or at least very hard to achieve. One could imagine a zealous humanist trying to construct some secular analogue for morning prayer, or for grace before meals. But the most likely result of such endeavours, I predict, will be something flat and indigestible – a formula that merely asserts 'Well, it's nice that I am still alive for another day of potential activities that may be worthwhile for myself and others'; or 'It's good that we are about to sit down to a nice meal, and it's ethically useful to remember that much work was necessary to enable this nutrition to be made available to us.' It is not that such views are devoid of value, or that it would be pointless to utter them, but that their thinness, their lack of the power and resonance given by a rich interpretative context, means they cannot capture a great deal of what is valuable in their theistic analogues. Just as a sober and unbiased assessment of one's merits leaves out much of what is valuable about the virtue of humility, and just as a purely aesthetic admiration of a fine sunset fails to capture what is meant by a sense of awe, in the same way such 'humanistic' analogues for prayer and praise seem to be woefully lightweight vehicles for carrying

---

[35] L. R. Kass, *The Hungry Soul: Eating and the Perfecting of Our Nature* (New York: Macmillan, 1994), pp. 228–31. See further J. Cottingham, *On the Meaning of Life*, pp. 97ff.

the weight of intellectual and affective response conveyed by the formulae of traditional spiritual praxis.

We have by now reached a heterogeneous range of reactive responses – humility, hope, awe, thankfulness – which have been identified as attitudes without which human life would be the poorer. A religious framework of interpretation provides a secure home for these attitudes, by offering vehicles for their systematic and regular expression, and allows them significance by incorporating them into a recognized schema of virtuous praxis. To the objection that the atheist could construct valid secular analogues of these responses I have argued that such a task, though theoretically possible, carries a serious risk of filtering out precisely what gives them depth and significance. And in practice, it may be added (albeit at the risk of generalizing into risky empirical territory), most atheists are unlikely in the first place to be tempted to investigate the possibility of alternative secularized forms of spiritual praxis. Atheism is most characteristically linked to a 'no-nonsense' rationalistic and sceptical kind of outlook, and a great many of its adherents are likely to condemn or discard the whole notion of spirituality as part of an untenable supernaturalist world picture.[36] So the upshot is that in the absence of morning prayer, one will simply get up in the morning and start the day; in the absence of a habit of saying grace, one will simply pick up the knife and fork and start eating. These, and many other differences in habitual patterns of behaviour and affective response give us, I am arguing, a more significant indicator of the difference between atheism and theism than if we focus on the abstract metaphysical claims. The mindset of the atheist is primarily different from that of the theist in virtue of its lack of a characteristic framework of hermeneusis and praxis, a framework which there is reason to regard as enriching the life of those who adopt it.

---

[36] A worldview which fits neither in this 'no-nonsense' camp nor in the theistic category is the Buddhist religion, which (in its prevailing form) is non-theistic, yet finds an important place for spiritual praxis. In a recent study that is highly sympathetic to the Buddhist outlook, David Cooper speaks of forms of Zen praxis as 'allowing things to be experienced as the "gifts" they are'. (*A Philosophy of Gardens* (Oxford: Oxford University Press, 2005), p. 158). It is unclear, however, how a framework of interpretation that views the world as an impersonal flux could find a genuine place for the kinds of affective response associated with, for example, saying grace: it is significant that Cooper feels obliged, in the passage just cited, to put the word 'gifts' in inverted commas.

5. Metaphysical freight revisited

It is by now perhaps long overdue to come back to the question of theistic *belief*. Although I have been stressing hermeneutic and practical aspects of theism, the most obvious point that a critic might raise is that the relevant frameworks of interpretation and ethical praxis all surely *presuppose* a belief in God. And hence so far from being an alternative way of distinguishing the theist from his opposite number, any reference to such frameworks already implies that the theist must be prepared to, and indeed is logically required to, assert at least one crucial metaphysical proposition which the atheist denies – that God exists.

Perhaps that is right – and I have already noted that the purpose of this paper is not to dispute that such a truth-claim is part of theism. But I want to conclude this paper by pointing very briefly to some crucial aspects of religious understanding that make this focus on the doxastic freight of theism surprisingly unhelpful.

A metaphysical belief of the kind we are now considering has a peculiar status from an epistemic point of view. Firstly, there have been widespread philosophical reservations since the time of Hume and Kant about the viability of the traditional proofs of God's existence. I do not take that issue to be finally settled, but let us assume for the purposes of the present argument that these reservations are well founded. Second, because metaphysical claims about God refer to a supposed transcendent entity that is wholly other than the natural world, there are, even if we can achieve some understanding of how such a mode of existence could be humanly conceived, considerable difficulties as to how it could then be established in any way remotely comparable to that used to establish a scientific hypothesis. Again, let us take it for the sake of argument that such difficulties are resistant to solution. What kind of epistemic warrant, then is left for the theist? A possible answer, which I wish to suggest as worthy of consideration (though I cannot argue for it properly here) is that intimations of the divine presence might be available, not universally, or in the detached context of dispassionate scientific scrutiny, but only to those in an appropriate state of trust and receptivity.[37] There are,

---

[37] See Cottingham, *The Spiritual Dimension*, esp. Chs 1, 6 and 7, for a development of this theme. Compare Paul Moser, 'Cognitive Idolatry and Divine Hiding', in D. Howard-Snyder

it is worth noting, many truths, quite outside the context of religion, which are subject to such accessibility conditions: truths about the trustworthiness and loving responsiveness of a spouse or partner, to take one quite significant example, can never be disclosed or accessed from a position of cold sceptical assessment, but only as part of a process of trust and commitment.

In the light of this, the objection that theistic praxis *presupposes* belief in God turns out to be radically misleading. It invites us to suppose that preparedness to assent to a metaphysical proposition about the existence of this divine supernatural entity is a *prerequisite* for embarking on the path of spiritual praxis. Yet it may turn out instead that intimations of the divine are available only to those who are prepared and trained, through such praxis, to approach God in humility and awe, to risk the vulnerability of trust and hope where there is no 'external' epistemic warrant or prior demonstrative certification, to express that thankfulness and praise for the gift of life which would be out of place were there no one and nothing to thank, to live one's life in the faith that such thankfulness does find a response, and is returned in joy and blessing. Only then may it be possible to glimpse those fleeting intimations of the divine, which must otherwise remain hidden. And even should they appear, there will be good reason to expect that, for most people, they will never have the character of irresistible certitude; for just as a loving parent will forebear to occupy all the space of a young child's helpless dependence and devotion, so that infinitely greater being, whom 'no man could see and live'[38] could not in love overwhelm his creatures but must remain glimpsed 'darkly' or 'mysteriously', 'as through a mirror'.[39]

Warranted assent to a metaphysical truth about the divine existence thus cannot be a precondition for theistic hermeneusis and praxis. And remember that such a truth is in any case at the very edge of human comprehensibility, like the immense mountain which, as Descartes put it, we can never mentally grasp, or put our arms around, though we may still somehow reach out and touch

and P. K. Moser (eds), *Divine Hiddenness* (Cambridge: Cambridge University Press, 2005), pp. 126–7: 'God can be all-loving in supplying evidence of God's existence in a manner sensitive to human receptivity to filial knowledge of God. We have no right to demand evidence of God's reality that fails to challenge us to undergo volitional transformation towards God's character. So God's hiding from a *casual* or *indifferent*, inquirer does not count against the reality of God's existence'.

[38] Exodus 33:20.
[39] *Blepomen gar arti di esoptrou en enigmati* (1 Corinthians 13:12).

it.[40] So the theist's position is less like that of one who has items of doxastic baggage carefully secured and stowed prior to the voyage, than of one who embarks on a journey of hope.

But if the goods are only glimpsed later in the voyage, if the whole purpose of the voyage presupposes there are indeed such goods, how can we responsibly embark? *Solvitur ambulando*: as children do, we figure out how to walk by walking. As Aristotle advised (in a secular context) we become virtuous by acting virtuously. We grow in knowledge and love of God by trusting God. That is what theism amounts to, and must, for human beings, amount to, for there is no other way. And as Pascal reminds us, the costs of the voyage are not so formidable that we risk great loss in embarking.[41]

---

[40] Letter to Mersenne of 27 May 1630.
[41] See Pascal, *Pensées* ed. Lafuma, no. 418.

3

PHILOSOPHY, THE RESTLESS HEART AND THE MEANING OF THEISM

John Haldane

Like to the Artick needle, that does guide
the wandering shade by his Magneticke pow'r,
And leaves his silken Gnomon to decide
the question of the controverted hour . . .
Ev'n so my soule, being hurried here and there
by ev'ry object that presents delights
Faine would be settled, but she knows not where . . .
Thus finding all the worlds delights to be but empty toyes
good God, she points alone to Thee.[1]

I

There is a style of philosophical argument designed to cast doubt on certain phenomena or purported realities, which takes the form of asking how things would differ if the items in question did not exist. How would our experience of the world differ if there were no abstracta or natural necessities? How would science be different if the hypothesis of plural but causally insulated and inaccessible worlds were deleted from speculation? How would human behaviour differ if there were no qualia? How would the world be different if there were no God?

Those who press such questions usually do so in a spirit of scepticism or eliminativism, and often with something like verificationism ready to hand: the general idea being that something that makes no discernible difference is no different from nothing at all. If experience would be the same with or without the abstract, or the necessary, or the phenomenal, or the divine, then these have no experiential content or effects; and what has no content or effects remains only in name.

[1] Francis Quarles, *Emblems Divine and Moral*, (1635) Bk 5, IV.

There are two broad responses to this sort of argument. The first involves accepting the challenge and trying to meet it on the terms in which it is posed. So one might try to show that qualia are implicated in explanations of perception or action. Or again, one might argue that the concept of the abstract is presupposed in the very idea of human experience inasmuch as this involves the classification of objects, and of experiences, by types; or that the necessary is presumed by certain kinds of subjunctive conditionals. Those familiar with the original challenges will know that these responses have counters to the effect that the proclaimed differences are in fact explicable in terms of lesser commitments, and know also that these counters in turn attract replies. And so it goes on.

The second kind of response involves refusing this dialectic by rejecting the terms of the sceptical argument, perhaps believing that to accept the challenge would be to endorse assumptions that would make it unassailable. If we conceive of something as non-empirical but then accept the demand to say how its existence or non-existence makes a difference to the empirically detectable, then we shall be in trouble, at least if we think of 'making a difference' in terms of sense-modification. Instead, we should refuse to allow the legitimacy of the challenge, or at least limit its scope. For while the demand that everything must be directly empirically discernible may be unreasonable, it may be proper to ask how the existence of the non-empirical might be registered or made theoretically plausible. And to the latter question there may be a variety of responses. Viewed in this way, challenge and response have a chance of doing more than simply standing in distant opposition.

I offer these observations to set the stage for what follows, since I am interested in the issues of what difference the existence of God, and the belief in God's existence might make to consciousness and reflection, and I will be considering the idea that common human experience leads to the expectation that there is a god, and that, in one way or another, the facts of this experience and consequent expectation themselves constitute evidence for the existence of the expected deity.

Arguments from experience to God are familiar enough, involving either encounters with purported natural or supernatural effects of God's activity. I shall be concerned, however, with less familiar reasoning: in this case from the *inclination* (spontaneous or elicited) to believe that there is a God, and from the *desire* for God. On initial consideration the fact of inclination or of desire might not be thought to confer any warrant on the claim that the inclined toward or desired for exists; but I shall argue that further reflection unsettles this negative estimate. In doing so I will be drawing on ideas suggested by Augustine, Aquinas, C. S. Peirce and C. S. Lewis; let me, therefore, quote briefly from each in turn.

Augustine: 'You arouse [us] to delight in your praise, for you made us for yourself and our heart is restless until it rests in you'.[2]

Aquinas: 'There is in every man a natural desire to know the cause of any effect that he sees; and from this arises wonder in men. But if the mind of a rational animal were unable to reach the first cause of things the natural desire would be in vain'.[3]

Peirce: '. . . a latent tendency toward belief in God is a fundamental ingredient of the soul, and far from being a vicious or superstitious ingredient, it is simply a natural precipitate of meditation upon the origin of the Three Universes'.[4]

Lewis: 'Creatures are not born with desires unless satisfaction for these desires exists. A baby feels hunger; well, there is such a thing as food. A duckling wants to swim; well, there is such a thing as water. Men feel sexual desire; well, there is such a thing as sex. If I find in myself a desire which no experience in this world can satisfy, the most probable explanation is that I was made for another world'.[5]

II

Philosophical reflections on the 'meaning' of theism typically take the form of analysing its conceptual or propositional content. Let

---

[2] 'tu excitas ut laudare te delectet, quia fecisti nos ad te et inquietum est cor nostrum donec requiescat in te'. *Confessiones*, 1. 1. 1.

[3] 'Inest enim homini naturale desiderium cognoscendi causam, cum intuetur effectum; et ex hoc admiratio in hominibus consurgit. Si igitur intellectus rationalis creaturae pertingere non possit ad primam causam rerum, remanebit inane desiderium naturae.' *Summa Theologiae*, Ia, q.12. a.1.

[4] 'A Neglected Argument for the Reality of God' in Charles Hartshorne and Paul Weiss, eds. *Collected Papers of Charles Sanders Peirce. Volume VI*, (Cambridge, Massachusetts: Harvard University, 1965), p. 333.

[5] C. S. Lewis, *Mere Christianity* (London: Fontana, 1960) Bk. III, chap. 10: 'Hope'.

us say, then, that theism is the position according to which there exists a single, ultimate, transcendent, immaterial cause of nature; a creative and sustaining agent antecedent to and independent of its effects; and which is all present, all powerful, all knowing, and all good. That is the sort of 'thing' about whose possibility, let alone actuality, much has been said and written. It is less common in contemporary philosophy to find reflections on the significance of theism; by which I mean the implications of it for our view of ourselves and our place in the scheme of things. D. Z. Phillips and other Wittgensteinians have long charged metaphysicians with treating the possible existence of God as if it were a purely speculative hypothesis. There is justice in that complaint. On the other hand it can seem that philosophers who focus on religious practices such as prayer and worship typically do so in ways that leave unanswered the question of whether those practices have any transcendent correlate. But because a hermeneutical and existential interest is appropriate it does not follow that a metaphysical one is excluded, and an adequate treatment of theism should aim to marry, at the level of understanding, religious practice and philosophical theology.

There is a parallel here with philosophy more generally. Contemporary epistemology and metaphysics often proceed as if they were forms of abstract information theory and micro-engineering. This leaves entirely untouched the question of wisdom, let alone the love of it; and it even makes puzzling how philosophy could have any special bearing on the nature of human existence. On the other hand, those who treat philosophy as if it were a branch of imaginative literature dedicated to the exploration of the psyche or of culture, with an option in edification (or misery), leave much of thought and reality unexamined, and they often miss the point that reality is, or should be, a measure or arbiter of human conduct. Again, what is most needed are not further rounds from either side, but the methodological insight that speculative and practical approaches are complementary, for though individually necessary they are only jointly sufficient.

These points are relevant to the present enquiry because it is a common human experience to have philosophical and religious thoughts and desires, to be moved by them, and to wonder whether they are responses to some reality. In reflecting on such states of mind we might speculate about their source, seek their confirmation, and in probing reality for the latter also look for something that could bestow meaning on life. These may appear no more than psychological observations, but there is an extended line of reasoning developed by Peirce which holds that something of the sort points to the existence of God.[6] Of this he writes:

> we should naturally expect that there would be some Argument for His reality that should be obvious to all minds, high and low alike, that should earnestly strive to find the truth of the matter; and further, that this Argument should present its conclusion, not as a proposition of metaphysical theology, but in a form directly applicable to the conduct of life, and full of nutrition for man's highest growth.[7]

The 'Neglected Argument', as Peirce terms it (meaning to refer to its neglect by theologians) draws on a number of distinctions. First, on the side of thinking: between *argument* understood as 'any process of thought reasonably tending to produce a definite belief', and *argumentation* denoting structured reasoning 'proceeding on definitely formulated premisses'. Second, as among the correlates of thought: between three categories which Peirce terms 'Universes of Experience'. The first of these universes is the world of 'Ideas' or concepts, considered as thinkable contents, whose reality ('Being') consists 'in mere capability of getting thought' (p. 312). The second is the 'Brute Actuality of things and facts', in which events occur in primitive relations of de facto consequence and exclusion. Of these things and facts Peirce writes that 'their Being consists in reactions against Brute forces'. Finally, there is the world of 'Signs' or intentional and more broadly teleological phenomena. The Being of these, according to Peirce 'consists in active power to establish connections

---

[6] It is a significant mark of change within philosophy that whereas earlier writers on Peirce discuss this aspect of his work with interest, more recent ones either ignore it or treat it as something of a departure from otherwise rigorous thought. In his generally very good study, *Peirce* (London: Routledge & Kegan Paul, 1985), Christopher Hookway registers his own puzzlement writing 'Presumably, an inquiry which shows us the reality of God must not be motivated by *practical* concerns; it must be a theoretical inquiry. But it is hard to see what theoretical question could call for the hypothesis of God. These and other similar considerations, make us sympathetic to those like Goudge who point to Peirce's writings on religion to support their view that his writings show us a man torn between competing and inconsistent intellectual directions' p. 277. I hope the present essay might serve to challenge this comment.

[7] Op. cit., p. 457.

between different objects, especially between objects in different Universes' (op. cit.).

This last category is, like much else in Peirce's presentation, obscurely characterised. He offers as examples a living consciousness, a plant's power of growth, a living (political) constitution, a daily newspaper, a great fortune and a social movement. One might, however, think of the category as conforming in part to the traditional Aristotelian definition of soul as the principle of activity or first actuality of something (an organised 'body') that serves as the natural instrument of that power or capacity (*De Anima* 412). Accordingly, the human body is animated by the rational soul, a plant by its individual vegetative nature, a polity by its constitution, a newspaper by its editorial principles, a mass of wealth by its operating schemes of accumulation and disposal, and so on. Similarly, I suggest that Peirce's various characterisations of the reality of members of the three Universes corresponds broadly to Plato's criterion of existence as possessing any kind of power to affect, or to be affected by another (*Sophist* 247). Ideas are *thinkable*, brute actualities *react*, and signs *connect*; and in general Universes are domains of entities characterised by powers and liabilities.

The 'Neglected Argument' has as its first stage what Peirce refers to as the 'humble argument'. Allow one's mind to engage in *musement*: disinterested and unregulated contemplation; thought playing freely over nature and consciousness, observing patterns, parallels, counterparts, analogies and regularities, and proceeding to conclusions from these. Beginning as pure receptivity reverie settles into focussed observation, and from that to musing, and hence to the unforced hypothesis that behind the natural and mental phenomena lies a common source: God. Beyond this stage of reasoning lies the 'neglected argument' proper, in which the efficacy of the previously naturally arising hypothesis is assessed and vindicated. A spontaneous belief in God, undirected and near to universal, is recognised to have implications: a speculative hypothesis becomes a demand on one's life. From having been moved to posit God as the source of order one proceeds to consider what the practical import of this might be; and in thinking this through a disengaged speculation becomes a settled and demanding state of belief. Peirce writes:

> Any normal man who considers the three universes in the light
> of the hypothesis of God's Reality, and pursues that line of

reflection in scientific singleness of heart, will come to be stirred to the depths of his nature by the beauty of the idea. . . . Now to be deliberately and thoroughly prepared to shape one's conduct into conformity with a proposition in neither more nor less than the state of mind called Believing.[8]

From this stage of engaged reflection one proceeds to the third argumentative phase in which both the affirmation of God's existence and its practical implications are examined. Several modes of inference have come into play: first, *abduction* (abstractive induction), and *retroduction* which are related forms of argument (not argumentation) by which one intuits or infers to the best explanation of the phenomena, then *deduction* involving explication of the hypothesis and derivation of its entailments, and *induction* through which derived ideas are connected to experience.

Cutting through Peirce's terminology, the line of argument is easily stated. Left to their own devices human beings move through several cognitive stages in which they proceed from 1) registering things as unaligned and unregulated, to 2) seeing them as connected, though not yet intelligibly so, to 3) discerning order in the domain of consciousness and in that of its presumed objective correlates. This cognitive development induces an inferential one, for as order comes into view so too does the natural hypothesis of an ordering source; and that hypothesis having been proposed it may be subjected to practical and scientific testing.

If there really is a God behind the phenomena, then that fact should serve to make sense of various speculative and practical impulses towards philosophy, science and art, to personal relations, and towards awe, reverence and worship. It should also explain the experience of order, including the order of our own increasingly probative and abstract reasoning. Peirce's originating argument is that when we step back from immediate concerns and let our minds go into the kind of receptive but disinterested free-play that Kant appealed to in explanation of the aesthetic, we find ourselves discerning order and dependency of which we are not in general the authors, and on the strength of that insight we spontaneously come up with the idea or insight of a transcendent source. As Peirce puts it:

---

[8]   Op. cit., p. 467.

In the pure play of Musement the idea of God's Reality will be
sure sooner or later be found an attractive fancy, which the
muser will develop in various ways. The more he ponders it, the
more it will find response in every part of his mind, for its
beauty, for its supplying an ideal of life, and for its thoroughly
satisfactory explanation of his whole threefold environment.[9]

The Neglected Argument is experiential but unusually so. It is
not focussed upon a special class of religious phenomena, or
upon a distinctive sense of the numinous, but on experience
quite generally as defined over the three Universes; and
although in its later stages it invites us to test the explanatory
hypothesis against scientific observations, it is not in the ordinary sense an argument from design, though it shares features
with that as with cosmological arguments. Rather it is, thrice
over, an inference from observed existents and structures to the
best explanation of these: first, intuiting that the best explanation of seeming being and order is actual being and order;
second, recognising that the best explanation of order is an
orderer; and third, arguing that the best explanation of our
observing order and postulating an intelligent cause of it is that
we were intended to do so by a God who wanted us to know of
Him. This last point is of broader interest and will be taken up
again in the next section when I discuss not the inclination
towards theistic belief, but the desire for God.

Clearly many questions might be posed to Peirce's argument.
I will touch on some general issues in conclusion, but for now
I suggest that readers follow the same procedure as Peirce
describes. If he is right then human kind has a natural tendency
upon free reflection to conclude 1) that there is order in the
various Universes, for which he is not responsible; 2) that the
best explanation of this is the existence of a transcendent cause
or order; and 3) that this cause has bestowed upon us the cognitive powers required for observing evidences of it, and for
inferring from these its continuing efficacy. In short, our natural
inclination consequent upon experience to believe in God is
indeed evidence of God's existence, both in respect of the
epistemic grounds of that inclination, and on account of its very
existence.

---

[9]   Op. cit., p. 465.

III

The quotation from C. S. Lewis comes from a discussion of the theological virtue of hope in which he suggests that, given serious self-reflection, most people would acknowledge that what they aspire to most acutely is something that the world does not provide. Lewis then describes three responses to the disappointment felt with the goods of this world. First, that of the Fool, who dismisses these simply as bad specimens, and goes looking for better ones. Second, that of the disillusioned Sensible Man, who recognises that further searching will only result in repeated disappointment, and so concludes that it was a mistake to seek for better than the mundane. Last is the response of the religious believer who argues, as in the quoted passage, that natural desires are not in vain, and hence that the longing for deeper satisfaction than this existence can offer, points to another world within which fulfilment may be found.[10] This last response suggests the following argument:

1. Every natural desire has a corresponding object, the attainment or experience of which constitutes that desire's satisfaction.
2. There is a natural desire for transcendent fulfilment, which cannot be attained or experienced in the present world.
3. Therefore,there exists that which constitutes the satisfaction of the natural desire for transcendent fulfilment, but this satisfier lies beyond the present world.

Neither Lewis's discursive reasoning nor this argument refers immediately to God as the end of transcendent desire, but the original discussion makes it clear that what is at issue is a beatific afterlife, more precisely a Christian notion of 'Heaven' as involving union with God 'in eternity shar[ing] His splendour and power and joy' (op. cit). So let me add as follows:

4. God is, or is an essential condition of the satisfaction of the natural desire for transcendent fulfilment.
5. Therefore, God exists.

---

[10] Lewis rehearses a similar argument in 'The Weight of Glory', a sermon delivered in 1942 and gathered in C. S. Lewis, *The Weight of Glory and Other Addresses*, (ed.) W. Hooper (New York: Harper Collins, 2001).

Evidently there is scope for further explication of terms and premises. For example it might be observed that in 4. God is postulated as a condition of satisfaction in a future other world, and hence that it does not follow that he exists antecedently in the present world. I leave it to readers to consider which aspects of the divine nature might most economically be invoked to deal with this point, e.g. by reference to necessary existence, eternality or universal creation. Likewise it might be queried whether even if there is a satisfier of the natural desire for transcendent fulfilment this needs to be or be provided for by God. I shall return to this point later but more pressing are issues concerning the plausibility of the first two premises.

(1) *Whether every natural desire has a corresponding real object, its satisfier.* Clearly not every desire has an actual satisfier answering to the description of the intentional object of that desire. One of the marks of intensional contexts is failure of existential inference and generalisation. The truth of 'John desires to ascend a golden mountain' does not entail the existence of a particular golden mountain, or of golden mountains in general. Yet some content has to be given to the conception of the desired object and it might be argued, in the style of a compositional semantics for intentional contents, that the primitives out of which 'golden mountain' is composed do, and must have extensions. Even if this were true, however, it would not follow that the composite concept does, and it would be false to claim as a matter of implication that whoever wants what is specified by a composite description wants, and hence would be satisfied with, its component elements.

A better line of thought lies in the direction of distinguishing natural and artificial desires. Under the influence of others, or through encounter with cultural representations one may form desires that would not otherwise arise. A longing for an iPod or MP3 player is an induced, culture-dependent desire. These objects exist but other artificially induced desires may lack correlates. For entertainment or mischief, someone might conjure up the idea of a type of (non-existent) object or situation and then promote it as a desirable end. In consequence, a desire may become widespread that has no satisfier. Setting aside the earlier compositional theory, one might try arguing that any such desire is specifiable in terms of some other description of its object, and that under some such alternative description it has a relevant correlate. So the person wanting a flying car, say, is really wanting an unusual, high-technology transporter, or an object of awe to others; and there are certainly real things that might satisfy his desire so re-specified. As before, however, this risks misrepresenting the character of the originally identified desire. Moreover to the extent that a re-description strategy seems plausible it is likely to strengthen the case for distinguishing natural and artificial desires, and providing correlates for prima facie objectless members of the latter category by treating them as (*per accidens*) determinates of (*per se*) determinable natural desires. For example, the desire for a flying car may be a culturally dependent expression of a natural desire for power or status. By this point, then, it would be worth considering directly the idea that, whatever about artificial longings, every natural desire has an objective correlate. That claim will have to be understood as pertaining to types rather than instances: the desire for food has a real type of satisfier, viz, food, though no portion may be currently available. In the case of a desire for God or what is essentially God-involving, however, the distinction between available type and unavailable instance or portion is inapplicable. Two issues now arise: first, how might natural desires be identified? And second, what would explain their existence?

With regard to the first, there are three significant markers: 1) spontaneity of occurrence; 2) prevalence to the extent of normal universality; and, 3) common linguistic identification of types of desire and/or of their satisfaction, and/or of their deprivation.[11] The desire for food and sex occur without cultivation; are prevalent to the extent that their absence generally invites explanation; and natural languages have words for these desires and/or for their fulfilment and/or their frustration. By contrast, artificial desires are 1) acquired or inculcated; 2) liable to be non-universal and culturally variant; and 3) not ubiquitously linguistically represented. In these terms the desire for transcendence has a good claim to be a natural desire. Determining how widespread it may be is, of course, dependent upon having a characterisation of it, and what has been given so far is admittedly abstract and indeter-

---

[11] I note in passing that among the marks of 'first principles' of knowledge, according to Thomas Reid, are their universality, their representation in all languages, their early appearance antecedent to instruction, and their practical necessity. See Thomas Reid, *Essays on the Intellectual Powers of Man* (ed.) D. R. Brookes (Edinburgh: Edinburgh University Press, 2002), Essay VI, Of Judgement.

minate; but like Peirce's hypothesis of an ordering source that
may be the nature of the phenomenon in its initial manifestation.
Allowing for this provisional indeterminacy, the impulse to seek
transcendent fulfilment is testified to in a whole range of cultures
and correspondingly is detectable in language, such is the basis
for the prominence of religion as an area of study within cultural
anthropology.

Setting aside for a moment the particular question of whether
the desire for religious transcendence is indeed a natural desire,
so as to address the broader issue of the existence of such
desires understood as being ones that have objective correlates
(at least at the level of instantiable types), there are two obvious
accounts of their occurrence: God or nature. A providentialist
will say that God has designed us so as to have an innate desire
for what we need for our fulfilment, and has provided satisfiers
of those needs. An evolutionary naturalist will say that our
innate desires are adaptive and confer reproductive advantages.
Animals that had no desire for food or sex, or who had such
desires though there was no possibility of their fulfilment would
not long have survived. Our survival over innumerable generations is testimony to the utility of innate and satisfiable desires.
Favouring the providentialist explanation in this context would
render the broader argument gratuitous; but while the natural-
istic alternative is not correspondingly pre-emptive nor does it
exclude a theistic explanation. After all, showing that some
feature has adaptive utility does not explain its existence, only
(*ceteris paribus*) its persistence-as-advantageous. So the providentialist and evolutionary accounts are compatible, and certainly
agree that there are natural desires and that there is a presump-
tion that they have satisfiers.

(2) *Whether there is natural desire for transcendent fulfilment.* I
have already claimed that there is a good case for the desire for
transcendence being a natural longing. Beyond the anthropo-
logical and linguistic evidence for this there is also personal testimony and phenomenological reflection including that arising
from the musement described by Peirce. Writing in mid-
life to two female intimates Bertrand Russell observed the
following:

> The centre of me is always and eternally a terrible pain . . . a
> searching for something beyond what the world contains, some-
> thing transfigured and infinite – the beatific vision, God – I do

not find it, I do not think it is to be found – but the love of it is my life . . . it is the actual spring of life within me.[12]

Even when one feels nearest to other people, something in one seems obstinately to belong to God and to refuse to enter into any earthly communion – at least that is how I should express it if I thought there was a God.[13]

One could easily multiply serious reflections of these sorts, though against them would have to be set the testimony of self-avowedly godless minds. Moving to the larger scale, however, it is evident that religious aspiration and commitment is extensive even if there is scope for querying the relationship between this and the longing for transcendence – though recall that for the latter to exist it need not be self-ascribed under that or some conceptually equivalent description. The concept or, if one prefers, the 'phenomenon' of religion is evidently somewhat indeterminate. It has paradigm instances, less clear cases and progressively more doubtful ones. Even restricting oneself to more or less clear instances, however, there are vast numbers of religious believers throughout the world. Indeed, of the six and a half billion humans on the globe about eighty percent belong to recognised religions. Arguably nothing compares with religion as a domain of commitment. What then explains the origins of religion and its power to draw and to hold the longing and allegiance of so many?

Peirce's answer is that religion gives expression to a universal need to acknowledge and respond to an experienced sense of cosmic order and human 'creatureliness'. His is a transcendentalist version of an old thought: in writing that 'ever since the creation of the world [God's] invisible nature, namely his eternal power and deity, has been clearly perceived in the things that have been made' (*Romans* 1: 19–20), St Paul was expressing an idea already familiar to him prior to his Damascene conversion. A century beforehand, Cicero wrote 'what can be so obvious and clear, as we gaze up at the sky and observe the heavenly bodies, as

[12]   Bertrand Russell, Letter to Colette O'Neil (Lady Constance Malleson) October 23, 1916 from *The Selected Letters of Bertrand Russell: The Public Years 1914–1970*, (ed.) N. Griffin (London: Routledge, 2001).
[13]   Letter to Gladys Rinder August 11, 1918. from *The Selected Letters of Bertrand Russell: The Public Years 1914–1970*, (ed.) N. Griffin (London: Routledge, 2001) p. 148.

that there is some divine power of surpassing intelligence by which they are ordered' (*On the Nature of the Gods* Bk. 2, 4). Earlier still and in other cultures the idea of a transcendent source of existence, order and movement seems to have been prevalent. Another possibility is that religion originates in an innate longing. Experiences of wonder may elicit it, but it is not a conclusion derived from them. Rather we have inbuilt within us a desire for transcendence, a notion of a supreme other, and an attitude of awe or piety towards the world as the work of that 'Other'. Initially the idea might be embryonic and ill-defined, but given time it could grow into natural religion. And the religious orientation might, as Augustine supposed, have been put there by God himself – in order that we should have a good chance of coming to know and to love Him.

A third answer, which will return us to the perspective of the evolutionary naturalist, might conjecture that religion does indeed derive from an idea in our minds but that this idea has not been arrived at by our observing nature or ourselves, or been put there for a purpose; but instead is simply the result of an ancient accident of circumstance which has survived because it confers certain advantages. Suppose in other words that religion is a product of blind evolution. The problem with this, however, is that it fails to address the nature of religious aspirations and beliefs as *aspirations* and *beliefs*. What needs to be accounted for is why people actually hold to certain longings and ideas and engage in particular practices, and part of that explanation will involve their *beliefs* about the point and value of those religious notions and practices. The fact that ancestors behaving in related ways enjoyed certain reproductive benefits in consequence, hardly touches the issue.

In a recent book, Daniel Dennett presents the evolutionary case as follows:

> [R]eligion is a human phenomenon, it is a hugely costly endeavour, and evolutionary biology shows that nothing so costly just happens . . . the ultimate measure of evolutionary 'value' is *fitness*, the capacity to replicate more successfully than the competition'
> . . . The memorable nymphs and fairies and goblins and demons that crowd the mythologies of every people are the imaginative offspring of a hyperactive habit of finding agency wherever anything puzzles or frightens us. . . . The [myths] that

get shared and remembered are the souped-up winners of
billions of competitions for rehearsal time in the brains of our
ancestors'
. . . [religion] is a finely attuned amalgam of brilliant plays and
stratagems, capable of holding people enthralled and loyal for
their entire lives.[14]

His book is a brick (450 pages) possibly suitable for breaking
church windows – but was it designed as such? In dealing with
artefacts one needs to distinguish between intended purposes and
incidental effects. Dennett intended his book to be read not
thrown; but it can be thrown and its use as a missile might confer
reproductive benefits on those who so deploy it. The logic of
evolutionary explanations requires, however, that one discriminate between heritable adaptations that have been selected for
per se because of the advantages they confer, and incidental
by-products selected *per accidens*. It may have been the case that
objects of the rough size, shape and weight of Dennett's book
were used by his ancestors and are used by his contemporaries as
missiles. but that does not settle the question of the actual point of
the book. Is its being a book, or a potential weapon, an intended
or incidental feature of its manufacture? The answer is clear.
Similarly, whatever benefits may have attached, or attach, to
engaging in certain forms of behaviour, the question to address in
understanding religion is the meaning and value of that behaviour, and its associated beliefs and values, *as religious expressions*,
not as evolutionary adaptations. There is, as must be, a great deal
of pure conjecture in Dennett's speculations about our ancestral
past, but they are also besides the point so far as concerns the
obvious issues raised by religious claims and aspirations to transcendence, viz. what do they mean and are they true?[15]

So I return to the fact of billions of believers and to the suggestion that religion is a natural response to the universal sense of
being in a world created and governed, by what and to what end
one does not quite know. Whether that intimation of creation and
creatureliness is warranted is indeed a question for investigation,

[14]   Daniel Dennett, *Breaking the Spell: Religion as a Natural Phenomenon* (New York: Viking,
2006), pp. 69, 123–4, and 154.
[15]   Dennett does consider briefly whether religious beliefs might be true, (Ch. 8 sec 7:
'Does God exist?') but the discussion, barely six pages, takes the form of 'expressing my
own verdicts but not the reasoning that has gone into them' (p. 240).

but it requires attention to the content of religious claims and requires assessment of their plausibility. The spell of religion is the sense that those claims register something of the truth about the nature of human beings, their place in the cosmos and the significance of their lives. And the issue remaining is whether the pervasive fact of religious belief and desire itself points to a transcendent religious reality.

IV

Among my earlier brief quotations was one from Aquinas's *Summa Theologiae* (1a, q12. a2). It makes reference, as I have done, to a natural desire (*desiderium naturale*) and to the idea of God as providing its proper fulfilment. By that point in the *Summa*, however, Aquinas has already presented the 'five ways' (*ST.* 1a, q2, a3) and so is not arguing for, but presuming the existence of God. His issue is 'whether any created intellect can see the essence of God?' and his reasoning is that since God is the *causa prima*, and men have a natural desire to attain the ultimate cause, if they were unable to come to know the divine essence then their natural desire would be in vain. That outcome would be problematic for several reasons. It would mean that either men's fulfilment lies in something other than God, or that they are set to remain unfulfilled. Both possibilities run counter to Christian teaching about human dependence and destiny; but beyond that there would be the problem that since the desire is taken to be part of man's created nature, then God would have implanted a tendency that could not be fulfilled, and that would be incompatible with His goodness and reason.

The principle to which, I believe, Aquinas is committed and is operating with, namely that every natural desire has an objective correlate, can be seen as an instance of the general teleological principle that every created tendency has an attainable end, *finis* (*telos*). That principle is not as such a theological one, which is why I wrote that it would be counter to God's reason, as well to His goodness, to create a desire that could not be fulfilled. But if the principle is indeed a metaphysical one to the effect that the existence of natural desires is non-contingently related to the real possibility of their satisfaction, then Aquinas is in a position to use the fact of a natural desire for God to argue for the existence of God. But this he does not seem to do, or at least not directly in the way one might now imagine.

The simplest and most immediate 'desire argument' requires the premise that there is a desire for God; but that claim is ambiguous between extensional and intensional interpretations. By the latter I do not mean a reading according to which the only implied object is an intent(s)ional one (and hence any existential inference is invalid), but rather an interpretation which requires that the proper objective correlate of the desire is desired *as such*. The former reading by contrast allows that the objective correlate may be desired under some other description, such that substitution (of co-extensive terms) *salva veritate* may fail. Thus we have two possibilities:

(1) There is a natural desire for God identified as such; and
(2) There is a natural desire, the actual but unidentified proper object of which is God.[16]

What I described as the simplest and most immediate argument would deploy (1). yet this is what Aquinas does not do. Why not? The issues are complex and include ones that have divided Thomistic interpreters, philosophers and theologians.[17] They turn in part on a theory of the forms or degrees of knowledge of God: contrasting *general knowledge* which is highly imperfect, being both somewhat confused and incomplete; *philosophical knowledge* which though more refined is still partial and must proceed, at least in part, *via negativa*; and *intellectual apprehension* which involves knowing something of the essence of God through reflection on the knower's own intellectual essence. The last is still partial, for according to the principle that knowledge is had or received according to the condition of the knower, a finite mind has only finite knowledge. But it is nevertheless, clear, distinct and positive.

To this division of forms of knowledge has to be added the further claim that human desire is cognitive to the extent that it is always under a description and within an epistemic framework

---

[16] It is an interesting question, which I cannot now pursue, how far apart the content of a desire can stand from an object that satisfies it (in extension) and still be regarded as a desire for that object.

[17] See W. R. O'Connor, *The Eternal Quest: The Teaching of St. Thomas Aquinas on the Natural Desire for God* (New York: Longmans, Green and Co., 1947) and L. Feingold, *The Natural Desire to See God According to St. Thomas Aquinas and His Interpreters* (Rome: Apollinare Studi, 2001).

(however primitive). I do not barely desire x, but desire *x qua f*, attendant on certain beliefs, and so on. Accordingly, desire is subordinate to conceptual and epistemic attainment. Returning now to the desire for God, two possibilities are in view. First, that there is an innate rational desire for God: every human mind naturally desires *per se* the vision of God; and second, that there is a naturally elicited rational desire for God: every human mind that knows in some degree that God exists, naturally desires the vision of God under some conception.

Since the latter position presupposes some innate natural inclination it might be thought to favour the former as the relevant ground of the elicited desire; but the point about the subordination of desire to knowledge implies that one cannot have a desire for that of which one has no conception and about which one has no belief as to its existence. Certainly there is, as there must be, a relevant natural desire in the background to be brought into play. For Aquinas, however, it is not the innate desire to know God but the desire to *know*, i.e., to make sense of things and to understand their causes. That desire is progressive, pushing the agent forward from one stage to the next towards the ultimate ground and explanation. And since that *causa prima* is God, therefore God is the ultimate satisfier of the knower's natural desire. But how is the progression achieved? Barring the miraculous infusion of conceptual powers and knowledge, it comes through the inference from effects to causes, and precisely that inferential course is the procedure set out by Aquinas in the five ways. Famously, these are offered as establishing the thatness of God (as cause of change, order, etc) not as determining God's whatness (*quiddity*). Otherwise put, they provide extrinsic not intrinsic characterisations of God.[18]

Aquinas does not argue to God's existence from the natural desire for God, because that desire is a composite of a natural desire to know (an orientation towards understanding) and some specific descriptive knowledge (that there is a *causa prima*) achieved through causal reasoning. It is only when one knows that a first cause exists as the ultimate ground of being and order, a cause 'to which everyone gives the name God' (*quam omnes Deum nominant*, ST. 1a, q2, a3) that one can desire to be united with 'It';

---

[18]   For more on this see my contributions to *Atheism and Theism: second edition* (Oxford: Blackwell, 2004).

so a direct argument from desire would presuppose what it set out to establish. But that does not mean that natural desires are irrelevant to the case for God, since the existence of such desires implies the existence of their correlates, and that order of teleology, as well as the particular epistemic desire, is the sort of thing that calls for an explanation.

V

How in light of this stand the arguments of Peirce and Lewis from inclination and desire? Peirce's position fits well with that of Thomas. His Neglected argument, beginning with its Humble phase, conforms to Aquinas's picture of the human desire for knowledge spontaneously giving rise to abductive hypothesis, insights into the ground of various orders of existents. There being such a propensity is exactly what one would expect if we were creatures of a God who created us antecedently ignorant but with the appetite and capacity to know and to advance in knowledge to the source of things. In retrospect Lewis's argument can be seen to be similarly modest in its assumptions. He writes not of an explicit desire for God but of 'a desire which no experience in this world can satisfy'. That is not a cry from the womb but a (*via negativa*) reflection upon life in which desires and knowledge have been sorted and assessed. In other words it also is a product of experience structured by natural desires and conceptual attainments. Admittedly, Lewis appears to differ from Aquinas (as I have invoked him) in seeming to speak of a longing that is not obviously epistemic; but further reflection would diminish this difference by elaborating the content of Lewis's sense of "a desire which no experience in this world can satisfy" and by attending to what Aquinas has to say about other affective modes and their place in human fulfilment.

The arguments from the inclination to believe and from the desire for fulfilment do not stand apart from other lines of enquiry but inform and are informed by them. And what they serve to explain is the profound summative thought-cum-feeling expressed by Augustine when in *Confessions* he wrote 'you made us for yourself and our heart is restless until it rests in you'. Finally, with regard to the challenge 'how would the world be different if there were no God?' the response that now suggests itself is a combination of the two previously described: that is to say, first, pointing to features of what is experienced that are explained by the hypothesis of theism but otherwise go unaccounted for, and second, pointing to the very fact of a dynamic structure of thought and desire by which we are led both to incline towards belief and to desire that to which belief has inclined us: *like to the Artick needle . . . my soul points alone to Thee.*[19]

[19]   The writing of this paper was made possible by research support from the Institute for the Psychological Sciences. I am grateful to Dr Gladys Sweeney, Dean of the Institute, for facilitating this support.

4

WORSHIPPING AN UNKNOWN GOD

Anthony Kenny

From time to time opinion polls endeavour to assess the state of religious belief in the community. Pollsters ask their victims such questions as 'Do you read the Bible?' 'How often do you go to church?' and so on. I discover that by the criteria of the polls I come out as a religious believer. I read the Bible frequently; I attend church more than once a month (even if, these days, it is often to attend memorial services). But in fact I am not a believer, I am an agnostic. Perhaps what the polls show is that I am a devout agnostic. I want to explore in this paper to what extent that is a reasonable position to occupy.

Probably a substantial majority of philosophers in Great Britain in the last fifty years have been atheists of one kind or another. But perhaps this statement needs qualifying. If a poll-ster approaches a philosopher with the question 'Do you believe in God?' the answer may very well be 'Well, it depends on what you mean by "God".' But even if questioner and answerer agree on a meaning – e.g. an all-knowing, all-powerful, all-good being who created the universe – there may still be reluctance to give a yes/no answer.

One reason for the philosopher's reluctance may be that there is an ambiguity in saying 'I do not believe there is a God'. Someone who says such a thing may mean 'I believe there is no God': the speaker is a positive atheist, someone who positively believes in the non-existence of God. Or what is meant may be something less definite: 'I have no belief that there is a God': such a person is only a negative atheist, someone who lacks a belief in the existence of God. A negative atheist is an a-theist or non-theist in the sense of not being a theist or believer in the existence of God. But the negative atheist is not necessarily a positive atheist: she may lack not only a belief in the existence of God, but also a belief in the non-existence of God. If the question had been 'Is there a God?' she would not have answered 'yes' and she would not have answered 'no'; she would have answered 'I don't know'.

Within negative atheism there is a further crucial distinction to be made. Those who lack the belief in God may do so either because they think that the statement 'God exists' is meaningful but uncertain, or because they think that the sentence is not really meaningful at all. Thus, one of the most celebrated nineteenth-century atheists, Charles Bradlaugh, expressed his own atheism thus:

> The Atheist does not say 'There is no God', but he says 'I know not what you mean by God; I am without the idea of God; the word "God" is to me a sound conveying no clear or distinct affirmation.'

The belief that religious language is meaningless was to have considerable popularity among philosophers in first half of the twentieth century and up to the present day.

Those who fail to believe in God because they think that the truth-value of 'God exists' is uncertain may be called agnostic negative atheists, or agnostics for short. They are people who do not know whether there is a God, but think that there is, in this area, a truth to be known. Those who think that religious language is meaningless think that the sentence 'God exists' does not have any truth-value, even an unknown truth-value; they think there is no truth to be known here at all. To refer to this class of negative atheists we might use the (superficially paradoxical) expression 'positivist negative atheists', or, more concisely 'positivists'.

The name is appropriate because the most systematic endeavour to show that religious language was meaningless was made by the logical positivist philosophers in the nineteen thirties and by their successors after the second world war. The thesis that talk about God is in an important sense meaningless had as one of its best-known defenders Sir Alfred Ayer.

We should note that there is no room for dividing positive atheist into two classes in the way we have divided negative atheists. Someone who believes there is no God cannot say that religious language is meaningless: for if it is meaningless, his own utterance 'There is no God' is meaningless also. If 'God exists' lacks a truth-value, so does its negation.

There are, then, four positions which philosophers may adopt with respect to the proposition 'There is a God', as follows:

(1) It is meaningless and neither true nor false: Positivism.
(2) It is meaningful and false: (Positive) Atheism.

(3) It is meaningful and may be true or false: Agnosticism.
(4) It is meaningful and true: Theism.

The positivists based their position on the verifiability criterion of meaning: a statement has factual meaning, they claimed, if and only if it is empirically verifiable. But statements about God are not verifiable even in principle, they argued, and therefore they lack factual meaning.

Some theists have tried to defend the meaningfulness of religious language by saying that statements about God are in principle capable of empirical verification: they have appealed to religious experience in support of the existence of God. Many more have rejected the verifiability principle itself as being extremely implausible even outside the religious context. In my view, this is correct. But what I want to do in this paper is not to criticise the positivist position but to show how closely it resembles a powerful religious tradition. In centuries past theologians of unquestioned devoutness have maintained that God was ineffable, and indeed inconceivable. We humans, they maintained, cannot speak appropriately about God, and we cannot even think coherently about him. In a quite strict sense, it is impossible to use words about God. God is not something to be captured by human language.

The founder of this tradition of negative theology is commonly held to be Dionysius the Areopagite, who drew on neo-Platonic sources. The three thinkers, however, whom I shall use to illustrate the doctrine of divine ineffability are John Scotus Eriugena in the ninth century, Anselm in the eleventh, and Nicholas of Cusa in the fifteenth.

Scotus Eriugena gives an extremely restrictive account of the use of language about God. God is not in any of Aristotle's categories, so all the things that are can be denied of him – that is negative ('apophatic') theology. On the other hand, God is the cause of all the things that are, so they can all be affirmed of him: we can say that God is goodness, light etc – that is positive ('cataphatic') theology. But all the terms that we apply to God are applied to him only improperly and metaphorically. This applies just as much to words like 'good' and 'just' as to more obviously metaphorical descriptions of God as a rock or a lion. We can see this when we reflect that such predicates have an opposite, but God has no opposite. Because affirmative theology is merely metaphorical it is not in conflict with negative theology, which is literally true.

According to Eriugena, God is not good, but more than good, not wise, but more than wise, not eternal but more than eternal. This language, of course, does not really add anything, except a tone of awe, to the denial that any of these predicates are literally true of God. Eriugena even goes as far as to say that God is not God, but more than God. So too with the individual persons of the Trinity: the Father is not a Father except metaphorically.

Among the Aristotelian categories which, according to Eriugena, are to be denied of God are those of action and passion. God neither acts nor is acted upon, except metaphorically: strictly he neither moves nor is moved, neither loves nor is loved. The Bible tells us that God loves and is loved, but that has to be interpreted in the light of reason. Reason is superior to authority; authority is derived from reason and not vice versa; reason does not require any confirmation from authority. Reason tells us that the Bible is not using nouns and verbs in their proper sense, but using allegories and metaphors to go to meet our childish intelligence.

> Nothing can be said properly about God, since he surpasses every intellect, who is better known by not knowing, of whom ignorance is the true knowledge, who is more truly and faithfully denied in all things than affirmed. (*Periphyseon* [c. 860], 1)

Our knowledge of God, such as it is, is derived both from the metaphorical statements of theology and from 'theophanies' or manifestations of God to particular persons, such as the visions of the prophets. God's essence is unknown to men and angels: indeed, it is unknown to God himself. Just as I, a human being, know *that* I am, but not *what* I am, so God does not know what he is. If he did, he would be able to define himself; but the infinite cannot be defined. It is no insult to God to say that he does not know what he is; for he is not a *what*. (*Periphyseon*, 2)

In describing the relation between God and his creatures Eriugena uses language which is easily interpreted as a form of pantheism, and it was this that led to his condemnation by a Pope three and a half centuries later. God, he says, may be said to be created in creatures, to be made in the things he makes, and to begin to be in the things that begin to be. (*Periphyseon*, 1,12) Just as our intellect creates its own life by engaging in actual thinking, so too God, in giving life to creatures, is making a life for himself. To those who regarded such statements as flatly incompatible with Christian orthodoxy, Eriugena could no doubt have replied that, like all other positive statements about God, they were only metaphors.

Eriugena's work reaches a level of agnosticism not to be paralleled among Christian philosophers for centuries to come. But the constraints that he places on language about God are perhaps no greater than those placed by Saint Anselm, who is not commonly thought of as a spokesman for negative theology.

The premise of Anselm's ontological argument is that each of us, even the atheist, has the concept of God as that than which no greater can be conceived. From this premise, St Anselm offers to prove that God must exist in reality and not only in the mind. But it is not to be forgotten that he goes on to say that that than which no greater can be conceived cannot itself be conceived. God, in Anselm's definition, becomes the outer limit of conception, because anything than which something greater can be conceived is not God. God is not the greatest conceivable object; he is himself greater than can be conceived, therefore beyond the bounds of conception, and therefore literally inconceivable (*Proslogion* [1077–8]).

How can Anselm avoid the conclusion that the word 'God' is meaningless? How is it possible to know what a word means if what it means cannot even be thought about? If a thing is ineffable, what is one saying when one tries to identify the thing? Anselm attempts to make a distinction between understanding words and understanding the thing which they describe. But this distinction can only be effective if the things in question are to some extent describable and to that extent are not ineffable, as Anselm believed that God was.

Negative theology reaches a climax of agnosticism in Nicholas of Cusa's *De Docta Ignorantia*. No one since Socrates had emphasized so strongly that wisdom consists in awareness of the limits of one's knowledge. Brute ignorance is no virtue: but the process of learning is a gradually increasing awareness of how much one does not know. Truth is real enough: but we humans can only approach it asymptotically.

Truth does not admit of more or less, but stands absolute. Nothing other than truth itself can measure it with accuracy, just as a non-circle cannot measure a circle in its absolute being.

Our intellect, which is not truth, can never comprehend truth so accurately that there does not remain the possibility of infinitely more accurate comprehension. Our intellect is related to the truth in the way that a polygon is to a circle: the more angles it contains, the more like a circle it is, but it never equates to the circle even if its angles are multiplied to infinity. (*De Docta Ignorantia* [1440], 9)

What is true of the intellect's approach to truth in general is *a fortiori* true of its approach to the truth about God.

Cusa's paradigm of rational inquiry is measurement: we approach the unknown by measuring it against what we already know. But we cannot hope to measure the infinite, because there is no proportion between what is infinite and any finite thing. Every attempt we make to learn more about God reveals a new infinite gap between what we think and what God really is.

Our reason, guided by the principle of non-contradiction, proceeds by making distinctions. We distinguish, for instance, between great and small. But these distinctions are useless in inquiry about God. We may think, for instance, that God is the greatest of all things, the maximum. Certainly, God is something than which nothing can be greater. But God, who has no size at all, is also something than which nothing can be lesser. He is the minimum as well as the maximum. This is but one instance of a general principle: God is the union and coincidence of opposites. (*De Docta Ignorantia*, 1,4)

One of the pairs of opposites that coincide in God is the pair being/nonbeing: '[The maximum] no more is than is not whatever is conceived to be. And it no more is not than is whatever is conceived not to be. It is one thing in such a way as to be all things, and it is all things in such a way as to be no thing. And it is maximally thus in such a way as to be also minimally thus.' (*De Docta Ignorantia*, 1,4)

No doubt this all sounds very irrational. Cusa praises those philosophers who have distinguished between reason and intellect, regarding intellect as an intuitive faculty which can transcend the contradictions detected by reason. Literal language is incapable of grasping divine mystery: we must make use of metaphor and symbol. Cusa's own preferred metaphors were mathematical. If we take a finite circle and gradually increase its diameter, the curvature of the circumference decreases. When the diameter reaches infinity, the circumference becomes absolutely straight.

Thus a straight line (the maximum of straightness) is identical with an infinite circle (the minimum of curvature). Cusa's agnosticism goes further than that of his predecessors such as Eriugena. Cusa regards negative predicates as no less misleading than positive ones if they are applied to God. No name is apt for God. We cannot even call him 'The One', because for us oneness excludes otherness and plurality. If we exclude that exclusion, when calling God 'the One' what are we left with? We are still infinitely distant from naming God (*De Docta Ignorantia* 1, 24). If we really come to grips with this reality, our informed ignorance will become sacred ignorance. That is the best that we humans can hope for here.

What room is left, in negative theology, for belief in God at all? If God is inconceivable, does that not mean that the notion of God is self-contradictory, and God a nonsensical *Unding* which cannot exist? That would be so if conceivability were mere freedom from contradiction; but there are many reasons for thinking that non-contradictoriness is not identical with freedom from contradiction. A notion is conceivable only if it is free from contradiction: that much is sure; but Kant, Wittgenstein, and the positivists have suggested other, more stringent, criteria of conceivability. The conditions laid down by these philosophers seem unsatisfactory for reasons unconnected with theism; but they are right to say that freedom from contradiction is only a necessary and not a sufficient condition of conceivability.

If God is inconceivable, is it not self-refuting to talk about him at all, even if only to state his inconceivability? The paradox here is one which is familiar in other areas of philosophy too. Bertrand Russell gave currency to Berry's paradox, which invites us to consider the expression 'the least natural number not nameable in fewer than twenty-two syllables'. This expression names in twenty-one syllables a natural number which by definition cannot be named in fewer than twenty-two syllables. Clearly, to solve this paradox, we have at least to distinguish between different ways of naming. And the solution to the paradox of God, if there is to be one, must be found by insisting that while we can speak of God, we cannot speak of him literally, but only in metaphor.

If this is so, there cannot be any *science* of theology. The God of scholastic and rationalistic philosophy is full of contradiction. Even in talking about God we must not contradict ourselves. Once we find ourselves uttering contradictory propositions, we must draw ourselves up. We can perhaps seek to show that the contradiction is only apparent; we may trace back the steps that led to the contradictory conclusion, in the hope that minor modification to one of the steps will remove the clash. Or we may claim that the contradiction arises because metaphorical language has mistakenly been taken literally. The one thing we must not do is to accept contradiction cheerfully.

To say that we cannot speak literally of God is to say that the word 'God' does not belong in a language-game. Literal truth is truth within a language-game. Some philosophers believe that there is a special religious language-game, and it is in that game that the concept of God is located. I believe, on the contrary, that there is no religious language-game, and that we speak of God in metaphor. And to use metaphor is to use a word in a language game which is not its home.

I know of no philosopher who has described the paradox of talking about the inconceivable godhead with such precision as the poet Arthur Hugh Clough. Consider, as an example, his poem of 1851 *Hymnos Aumnos* ('a hymn, yet not a hymn'). Its first stanza begins with an invocation to the incomprehensible Godhead.

> O Thou whose image in the shrine
> Of human spirits dwells divine;
> Which from that precinct once conveyed,
> To be to outer day displayed,
> Doth vanish, part, and leave behind
> Mere blank and void of empty mind,
> Which wilful fancy seeks in vain
> With casual shapes to fill again.

The poem starts from the assumption that the place to look for God is in the individual's inmost soul. Attempts to give public expression to the God encountered in the soul yield only meaningless, self-contradictory utterances ('blank and void') or images unconnected with reality ('casual shapes').

The second stanza of the poem, which I omit, develops the theme of the impotence of human utterance to embody the divine. In the third the poet proclaims that silence – inner as well as outer – is the only response to the ineffable.

> O thou, in that mysterious shrine
> Enthroned, as we must say, divine!

I will not frame one thought of what
Thou mayest either be or not.
I will not prate of 'thus' and 'so'
And be profane with 'yes' and 'no'.
Enough that in our soul and heart
Thou, whatso'er thou may'st be, art.

The agnosticism is radical: the *via negativa* is rejected as firmly as the *via positiva*. Not only can we not say of God what he is, we are equally impotent to say what he is not. The possibility, therefore, cannot be ruled out that one or other of the revelations claimed by others may after all be true:

Unseen, secure in that high shrine
Acknowledged present and divine
I will not ask some upper air,
Some future day, to place thee there;
Nor say, nor yet deny, Such men
Or women saw thee thus and then:
Thy name was such, and there or here
To him or her thou didst appear.

In the final stanza Clough pushes his agnosticism a stage further. Perhaps there is no way in which God dwells – even ineffably – as an object of the inner vision of the soul. Perhaps we should reconcile ourselves to the idea that God is not to be found at all by human minds. But even that does not take off all possibility of prayer.

Do only thou in that dim shrine,
Unknown or known, remain, divine;
There, or if not, at least in eyes
That scan the fact that round them lies.
The hand to sway, the judgment guide,
In sight and sense, thyself divide:
Be thou but there, – in soul and heart,
I will not ask to feel thou art.

The soul reconciled to the truth that there can be no analogue of seeing or feeling God, that nothing can be meaningfully said about him, can yet address Him and pray to be illuminated by his power and be the instrument of his action. But does not this presume that God can after all be described: at least as a powerful agent who can hear our prayers?

At this point we need to pause and consider the nature of the speech-act that is prayer. Prayer is not, in itself, a statement about God; it is rather an address to God. Among recent Christian writers about prayer one of the most insightful was the late Herbert McCabe O.P., who discussed its nature in an essay in the posthumously published collection *God Still Matters*.

McCabe observes that in recent years there has been a certain embarrassment among the faithful about prayers of petition. People have become furtive about praying to pass an exam or praying that their wives may recover from a dangerous illness. They are only a little less unhappy about praying for large scale things such as world peace.

> Of course the real objection people make to petitionary prayer is that it looks like manipulation of God. Here is God just about to make it rain for the sake of the farmers and their crops around Clyst Honiton when he overhears the urgent prayer of the vicar who is running his garden party that afternoon and changes his mind. Then there is always the question whether the louder and lustier prayers of the farmers may make him hesitate again. The critics ask rather smugly how it is possible for God to satisfy everybody, to hear all prayers, since good people frequently want incompatible things. (p. 72)

This makes it seem as if prayer is a waste of time. McCabe accepts this conclusion and glorifies in it. Prayer, he says, is an absolute waste of time, it is non-productive and non creative. But it is a waste of time that is a sharing into the waste of time which is the interior life of the Godhead, the life of love between the persons of the Trinity.

This response will seem cogent only to believers, but McCabe is surely right that one cannot take petitionary prayer at its face value. This ought to come as no surprise to anyone sympathetic to the line of thought I have been developing. If sentences in the indicative about God cannot be literally true statements, sentences in the imperative addressed to God cannot be literal requests either. In either mood, language about God is more like poetry than any other form of speech.

Once again, Arthur Hugh Clough has given magisterial treatment to the paradox here. In his early poem *Qui Laborat Orat*, he seeks to spell out what is involved in addressing prayer to an ineffable God.

O only Source of all our light and life,
    Whom as our truth, our strength, we see and feel
But whom the hours of mortal moral strife
    Alone aright reveal!
Mine inmost soul, before Thee inly brought,
    Thy presence owns ineffable, divine;
Chastised each rebel self-encentered thought,
    My will adoreth Thine.
With eye down-dropt, if then this earthly mind
    Speechless remain, or speechless e'en depart;
Nor seek to see – for what of earthly kind
    Can see Thee as Thou art?
If well-assured 'tis but profanely bold
    In thought's abstractest forms to seem to see,
It dare not dare thee dread communion hold
    In ways unworthy Thee.
O not unowned, Thou shalt unnamed forgive,
    In worldly walks the prayerless heart prepare;
And if in work its life it seem to live,
    Shalt make that work be prayer.
Nor times shall lack, when while the work it plies
    Unsummoned powers the blinding film shall part
And scarce by happy tears made dim, the eyes
    In recognition start.
But, as thou willest, give or e'en forbear
    The beatific supersensual sight,
So, with Thy blessing blest, that humbler prayer
    Approach Thee morn and night.

The poem has appealed to many readers – Tennyson was among its first admirers. It has been applauded by the devout no less than the sceptic and it has subtleties which are worth attention. There is first the paradox, obvious and surely intentional, that a poem which appears to deny the propriety of addressing the Godhead in prayer is itself an explicit second-person address to God. What is the inward bringing of the inmost soul before God but that 'lifting up of the mind and heart to God' which is one of the traditional definitions of prayer? The poet, therefore, is not so much attacking the practice of vocal prayer, as urging the praying soul to be aware of the limitations of human prayer, even at the moment of uttering one.

The first two stanzas, in particular, in their majestic movement, could stand by themselves as a prayer that might be uttered without misgiving by a perfectly orthodox Christian. They would, no doubt, be most congenial to those traditions which have emphasized the inner light rather than the external revelation as the supreme source of our awareness of God. But the solemn rallentando forced by the alliteration of the last two lines of the first stanza makes the beginning of the poem remarkably apt for liturgical recitation.

The second pair of stanzas develop, now in a more radical fashion, the traditional themes of the spirituality and ineffability of God. Because God is spirit, he cannot be seen by human eye, nor pictured by any inner eye of the imagination. Because God is ineffable, his nature cannot be expressed in language, and therefore it cannot be grasped by any human thought however abstract. Thus far many theologians of the most orthodox kind would agree with the sentiment of the poem. But must the conclusion be that the inner eye must be cast down and the inner voice be silenced?

The ineffability of God is given by Clough a moral as well as a logical element. Man must not attempt to name God, as Adam named the animals; for naming is a claiming of power; When God named himself to Moses it was in a manner which was a refusal to give a name. To leave God unnamed, then, is not equivalent to disowning him; on the contrary it is to refuse to claim an ownership which would be blasphemous.

Devout agnosticism could not wish for a more eloquent expression.

5

'SEEKE TRUE RELIGION. OH, WHERE?'

Michael McGhee

1. 'The truly religious'

The difficulty of the question – what difference does it make to someone that they believe in God or don't believe in him – is grimly highlighted when we confront it with the answer we might expect from the London bombers. What is at stake is our *conception* of religious belief, that internal representation of religion which becomes the unexamined and often unconscious measure of what we take seriously and what we dismiss, of what we think *must* and what we think *cannot* be the case.

In the aftermath of the bombings the writer Hanif Kureishi wrote in the *Guardian*[1] that

> We no longer know what it is to be religious, and haven't for a while. During the past 200 years sensible people in the west have contested our religions until they lack significant content and force. These religions now ask little of anyone and, quite rightly, play little part in our politics.
>
> The truly religious, following the logic of submission to political and moral ideals, and to the arbitrary will of God, are terrifying to us and almost incomprehensible. To us "belief" is dangerous and we don't like to think we have much of it.

Kureishi's faintly parodic style distances him from these sentiments which are nevertheless a commonplace among secular liberal intellectuals. Two remarks stand out, that we no longer know what it is to be religious and that 'the truly religious' are terrifying to us and almost incomprehensible.

The loss of concepts involved in our no longer knowing 'what it is to be religious' infects and impoverishes our language, so that

---

[1] 'The arduous conversation will continue', Tuesday 19th July 2005.

even as we dismiss religion we unnoticingly dismiss what may have been truths expressed within it, and disregard its power to criticise just the phenomena we now take to define religion itself. This loss is shown in the readiness to describe those who are allegedly terrifying to us as '*truly* religious', since the epithet exhibits a restricted knowledge of the phenomena – and seems to base itself rather insecurely on the self-assessment of the zealots.

ii. The view that is attributed to 'sensible people' by Kureishi has been vigorously expressed by another metropolitan intellectual, A. C. Grayling, who writes that throughout history 'religions have been the most destructive and threatening of social phenomena, often irrational and frequently oppressive and violent.' He adds, for good measure, that religion is 'a frightful disease, the cancer of history'.[2] If there had not been two centuries of criticism by 'sensible people', one might be lured into thinking, 'we' would be 'religious' and therefore equally fanatical and zealous. There is plenty of history to support this conclusion. And yet we all know that it is was never entirely like that, just as we know that Islam is not entirely like that either, though one has the suspicion that what Kureishi delicately hints at is that the only reason that it *wasn't* or *isn't* entirely like that is because even religious people were on the whole too inert or sensible to take their religion entirely seriously.

After setting the causal arrow from religion to irrationality and violence (as though what passes for 'religion' is not itself a *symptom* of this underlying human condition) Grayling endorses a telling remark of Voltaire, that he loved the man who seeks the truth but hated the man who claims to have found it. This is intended to press home the point that the religious are defined by their unas-sailable certainty of conviction.

But to catch the proper accent and target of Voltaire's thought we need to understand this gulf between the favoured seeker after truth, and the one who claims to have found it. What we don't like about the latter is that their conviction is both unassailable and premature – we don't like their *mentality*. Voltaire's two characters seem to represent different stages of experience in the moral and spiritual life of human beings. But to justify such a claim we need to set out the distinctions which frame the very idea of a moral and

²   See A.C. Grayling, *The Mystery of Things* (London: Weidenfeld & Nicholson, 2004), p. 220.

spiritual life. One also has to accept, and it is a significant admission here, that not all will be in a position to acknowledge the distinctions, which is one reason, for instance, that Kierkegaard insists on the need for 'indirect communication' between teacher and pupil in the trajectory of the spiritual life. However, one should also recall that the point for Grayling of the Voltaire remark is that it identifies the religious mentality *as such* rather than one mentality within religion among others, just as for Kureishi it seems to be "belief" *as such* that is 'dangerous'. And yet what it so obviously identifies – though one has to wonder whether this comment can even be heard, or the implied distinction be taken seriously – is not *the essential religious mentality* but authoritarianism and the premature, inflexibly self-confident certitude of *a particular kind* of religious conviction – the inflammable and often apocalyptic mentality of the zealot – by contrast with something quite different, what I should want to call the well-tempered demeanour of the spiritually developed person.

iii. My thinking here has been prompted in part by a remark of the late Ayatollah Morteza Motahari, who wrote that the religious project involves *training* of 'the raw, natural self'.[3] It is not my intention to discuss Motahari's sobering and oddly familiar account of this training, but to seek to apply to religion an aspect of the Aristotelianism hinted at in his remarks. The idea of a raw, untrained self recalls Aristotle's discussion of *akolasia*.[4] This term is often translated as 'licentiousness' but the literal meaning is the state of being 'un-chastised', and it evokes the idea of someone who is unrestrained, impatient, unreflective, quick to take offence[5], intemperate, not to say *violent*, and therefore angry and even brutal, in the pursuit of their ends and the protection of their certainties. Perhaps this profile is wider than that indicated by Aristotle's *akolastos*, who is unduly distressed by the absence of his pleasures, but the term may serve perhaps as a metonym for a

[3] A close associate of Khomeini assassinated in the aftermath of the Islamic Revolution in Iran. See for example his *Sexual Ethics in Islam and in the Western World* most conveniently available in PDF format at: http://www.iranchamber.com/personalities/mmotahari/morteza_motahari.php, esp. Chapter 5, pp. 21–23.

[4] See Aristotle's *Nicomachean Ethics* trans J. A. K. Thomson, Harmondsworth: Penguin, e.g., Book 3, 1118b28–1119a20 (p. 138f).

[5] The taking of offence or quickness to anger seems to be characteristic of a certain kind of religious zealotry. It is interesting to contrast this with the Pauline thought (1 Cor 13) that 'love does not take offence'.

more general syndrome that afflicts the intellectual as well as emotional life.

This picture may suggest someone who is *amoral*, or unable to think morally when the satisfaction of their desires is at stake, but we need not read it only in that way. The ends of such a person can also be informed by ideals of justice and solidarity. Readers who have wondered how this relates to our topic may see the connection just here: – that the trajectory from a mental condition of *akolasia* to the well-tempered one of *sophrosune*, determines the spirit in which a religious tradition is appropriated, determines what is salient in it for such an agent – determines the spirit of belief *and*, since the topic is the meaning also of its *absence* – the spirit of *non-belief*. It seems to me that these polar mental conditions provide the particular spiritual environments congenial to distinctive formations and repudiations of what we misleadingly call 'faith', and which, for reasons to be spelt out later, I should prefer to call 'religious belief'. It is not "belief" that is dangerous, but a particular admixture of ideal, judgment and violence.

iv. But, to conclude this section, certain turns of phrase employed by Kureishi and Grayling coincide ironically with language used by John Donne who, in his youthful 1590s *Satyre III, Of Religion*,[6] issues the injunction and bleak question which form the title of this essay: '*Seeke true religion. Oh, where?*'

Whereas Kureishi seems to know what 'true religion' is and would have none of it, Donne *seeks* it and would have none of its counterfeits – which coincide with what Kureishi thinks of as 'truly religious':

> *Keep the truth which thou hast found; Men do not stand*
> *In so ill case here that God hath with his hand*
> *Signed kings blank charters to kill whom they hate,*
> *Nor are they vicars, but hangmen to fate.*[7]

But by what criteria does Donne judge what is false or counterfeit in religion? The evidence of these lines suggests he is clear-eyed about self-serving hypocrisy and corruption and can see injustice

---

[6]   See John Donne, *The Satires, Epigrams and Verse Letters*, ed W. Milgate, Oxford: Clarendon Press 1967.
[7]   ibid.

beneath the cover of the religious masquerade. In other words, one criterion is precisely this moral judgment, an aspect of 'finding the truth' in another sense than Voltaire's: '*keep the truth which thou hast found*' is not obviously the premature and dogmatic conviction that Voltaire rightly deplores, and the truth to be kept hold of is that religion measures human conduct and is not to be measured by kings. On the contrary, the tradition to which Donne appeals demands far more than the little Kureishi says it now asks of anyone, since it requires *parrhesia*, the perilous speaking of truth to power.

2. The idea of transcendence

Not only are there different *theologies* in the unfinished history of the theistic religions, but also roughly corresponding *mentalities*. The polar mental conditions I have mentioned, and the spirit in which a religious tradition is appropriated are related to this. A particular theology may jar significantly with and even impede the development of *sophrosune*, and this may be the creative impetus to a new theistic conception which may in its turn be re-appropriated in an alien and akolastic spirit.

The historic movement from one kind of theology to another is well recorded, but an early poem by Stephen Crane ironically illustrates the familiar progression:

> *The livid lightnings flashed in the clouds;*
> *The leaden thunders crashed.*
> *A worshipper raised his arm.*
> *"Hearken, Hearken! The voice of God!"*
> *"Not so," said a man,*
> *"The voice of God whispers in the heart*
> *So softly*
> *That the soul pauses,*
> *Making no noise,*
> *And strives for these melodies,*
> *Distant, sighing, like faintest breath,*
> *And all the being is still to hear."*[8]

---

[8]   From Stephen Crane *The Black Riders and other Lines* [1895] in *War is Kind and other poems* (New York: Dover, 1998).

I do not draw attention to it because it highlights a shift in theological understanding, but because it sheds light on *how* such a shift might occur at all. It reflects a progression towards a demeanour that has an impact on the moral sensibility within which a particular theology is lodged, and of which it is a possible expression. But by that token, such a demeanour and sensibility may survive the demise of any kind of theology at all.

This claim is crucial for the argument of this essay, since it implies that it is not 'belief in God[9] or its absence' that matters, but the underlying spiritual and moral conditions in which belief or its absence emerges. This is not straightforward, however. A certain moral sensibility may be a *condition* of the development of a particular theology but a deepening moral understanding, for example of the nature of love and forgiveness, may then develop *within* that theology as it is lived out in the confrontation with events.

Crane's second stanza describes a spiritually determinate state of mind well recognised in spiritual manuals. Thus, e.g., the Buddhist practice of *samatha* meditation aims to reduce the vitiating influence of the *klesas*, the fires of greed, hatred and delusion, in favour of states conducive to insight, generosity and compassion. Crane's 'all the being is still to hear' define a *particular* spiritual atmosphere or environment in which a common *vision* of the world arises or is re-worked, an original apprehension, as it were, which is available to all but which, when not partaken of, is diluted into a received system of ideological belief.

ii. This is vague enough talk, but, for the moment, I should like to emphasise this latter point by alluding to Kant's insistence on autonomy of judgment. A genuine aesthetic judgment is grounded in *one's own* pleasure in the object and not someone else's. I cannot base a moral judgment on the authority of another for in such a case it is not genuinely a judgment that *I* make. By rough analogy, I only make a *religious* judgment when I apprehend or have a sense of something *transcendent*.

Now 'transcendence' is a term which needs to be treated with caution by readers of contemporary philosophy of religion. It is a relational term: if there is transcendence then some *x* transcends

---

An expression whose ambiguity will be discussed later.

(surpasses, goes beyond) some *y*. In the present case *y* is instantiated by 'the world' and one of our questions must be the determinability or otherwise of the *x* that allegedly goes beyond it (though indeterminability does not imply non-existence). 'The world' is not coterminous with 'reality' or 'what is', but is rather a limited whole, the ordered cosmos *within* 'what is'. The 'within' here gives us the essential container metaphor which determines our use of 'world'; it is as though we were always dimly aware of the possibility of a Platonic or Kantian intuition that the senses and understanding give us only a limited knowledge of what is there, that there are things beyond the world – beyond the Cave, which is the image of this uneasy intuition of containment. We enter the world and leave it, and there can be disturbing *irruptions* into the world and *eruptions* out of it. Sometimes we may have a vivid experience both of the limitations of the world and a sense of what lies beyond it, as when the young Wordsworth ties up his boat and leaves the lake, his brain working 'with a dim and undetermined sense/Of unknown modes of being'[10] – 'undetermined' just because they do not (yet?) belong to that determined part of reality that is incorporated into 'the world', and by contrast to which we see the world of our experience *as* limited at just the moment we see it as a limit that *it seems* can be surpassed.

My final focus in what follows is not, though, on the idea of something that lies beyond experience, beyond the senses and the understanding, *altogether*, but rather on a *determinable*, essentially moral transcendence, in which an uneasy intuition leads us to see the bondage of the passions as precisely and egocentrically limiting what we are able to apprehend.

Wordsworth's 'sense of something far more deeply interfused'[11] requires a comparative term, and this is a necessary aspect of the apprehension of transcendence: it is something more deeply interfused than the world we commonly inhabit and whose limits we sense just in this sense of a transcendent ground. The dyadic relation implied by 'transcendence' is incorporated into the experience of it: seeing the world as a limited whole is also and at the same time to have a sense of something beyond it, though, again, how we interpret that latter sense is another matter, though one of critical importance. The very idea of the world as a limited

---

[10] *The Prelude* [1850], Bk I lines 90–94.
[11] *Lines Composed a Few Miles Above Tintern Abbey*, line 94.

whole implies the idea of a position from which it is seen precisely
as that.[12]

iii. What is *common* to many traditions is just this sense of the world
as a limited whole, but what lies *beyond* the world is peopled,
mythopoeically or philosophically, in ways that seem to reflect the
moral as well as the cultural sensibilities of those who are subject
to these vivid apprehensions of the real condition of things. It is
for this reason that I stress that such a primal apprehension is
common also between the polar mentalities, *akolastic* and *sophronic*, that I have already mentioned. Although the theistic picture
is the dominant one within the traditions common to the inhab-
itants of our small island, there are other possibilities.

Within the Buddhist tradition one may become aware that the
world one perceives is determined by a restricted *parikalpita* consciousness, one which is eventually seen as a constricting construc-
tion of reality out of one's own desires, aversions and delusion,
in contradistinction, in the first place, to a more ample world
revealed when these desires are in abeyance, and, in the second
place, to the strange going beyond the conditioned world of
subject and object altogether.

It is in terms of the former case, however, that I want to place
the notion of a determinable moral transcendence, where the x
that transcends y is instantiated by a *life* released from bondage to
the destructive and egocentric passions ('the kingdom of heaven
is within you'), a life whose possibility is sensed as obscurely in the
first instance as any other 'unknown mode of being'. If the term
'transcendence' is a relational one, the apprehension of it is also
dyadic, since it involves both a looking beyond and a looking back,
as though when one *sees the world* one somehow sees it for what
it is and for the first time in graphic display, perhaps in some
exemplary scene or image. However we may seek in our philosophy and theology to populate what we take to go beyond the
world, we also envisage a position from which we can see that
world under the illumination of a perspective that was previously
unavailable. It provides us with the means of 'estimating' that
limited whole, as determined by greed, hatred and delusion, or by
the 'flesh'. The expression 'the world' which already seems to be

---

[12] I have sought to capture the sense of this notion of transcendence in 'Wittgenstein's
Temple: or How Cool is Philosophy?' forthcoming in *Philosophical Investigations*.

the remainder of a religious conception, carries all these reso-
nances, of what is both epistemologically and morally limited, as
the precipitate of a particular way of being and judging, a particular, determinate assimilation of such reality as is salient for the
urgent needs of a grasping subject.

iv. It is within the terms of these primal visions or apprehensions
of things, whose common denominator is the idea of a limited
world that can be transcended, that it seems to me that the notion
of 'religious belief' is best understood. Crane's attitude of listen-
ing and its concomitants is *one* of the background mentalities
within whose terms such a vision is *interpreted and understood*. What
I mean by that is that Crane's contrast, between the thunder and
the whisper of God's voice, amounts to a distinction *within* the
experience of seeing the world as a limited and conditioned
whole. To put it another way, this common vision by which we see
the world as a limited whole occurs against a determinate *moral* as
well as cultural background. The significant event in the poem,
then, is not its illustration of a shift in the concept of God, but its
highlighting of the different states of mind that determine what,
if we are disposed to think in such terms, our conception of God
will *be*, and, even if we are not so disposed, it preserves at least
some of the underlying attitude and its spiritual implications. The
moral sensibility – manifested in the particularity[13] not of language but of motive, intention and act – *drives* the theological
conception, and not the other way round. The historic change in
the theological conception towards the still small voice and the
God of Love looks like a creative outcome of an *ethical* pressure on
earlier conceptions that derives from an *independent* turning
around of interiority. The *akolastic* ('unregenerate') mentality dis-
regards or seeks to re-interpret such possibilities in terms of the
parameters of its own conception, driven by a mentality which is,
however, precisely an object of religious criticism from the perspective of the later, *sophronic* conception which is grounded in the
experience of the passage from the one condition to the other. A
critique and diagnosis of the *akolastic* mentality is written into the
sophronic self-understanding. What is significant here is that the

---

[13] I can never forget the unnerving comment in Kierkegaard's *The Concluding Unscientific
Postscript* (Princeton: Princeton University Press, 1968) that two people can believe themselves in agreement on the basis of their shared language and not suspect 'that an
agreement of this nature may be the grossest kind of misunderstanding' (p. 69).

new religious understanding offers a description and a kind of *vademecum* through the interior conditions of what becomes, in the Christian tradition, 'the life of the spirit' as it is contrasted with 'the life of the flesh'. Here we see a description of an alleged transcendence that is capable of being experienced. It is no accident that the 'flesh' (as opposed to the *body*) is often related to an ethical notion of the 'world' which refers to those whose perspective is determined by the preoccupations of the flesh. This life is claimed to be transcended by 'entering the life of the Spirit' or 'putting on the mind of Christ'.[14] Analogously, craving, aversion and ignorance, which constitute the condition of *samsara*, limit the perspectives available to us: the possibility of wisdom and compassion depends in the first place upon their temporary abeyance, and the state of *nirvana* is just the condition in which there is no further energy available for these states and they are 'extinguished'.

3. On being a believer

I have until now kept the term 'faith' in inverted commas, and I have done so because it shares a problematic ambiguity with the expression 'belief in God'. I shall come to the ambiguity in due course. But, as I have hinted, both are often conflated with 'religious belief' which is not just a more general term than either, but refers to something distinct from both of them.

'Faith' and 'belief in God' are deeply and specifically embedded and implicated in Abrahamic religious cultures. It is not obvious that they can be generalised over other traditions. Thus, to 'believe in God' is to manifest the theological virtue of *faith*[15], that is, to have, on the one hand, confidence in God's word and, on the other, to be faithful to it – hence, in the Judeo-Christian traditions, the significance of the image of a 'covenant', and in later, Christian, developments of this narrative, of 'redemption'. It is unfortunate, then, that the terms 'faith' or 'the faith' are sometimes used to refer to the particular form of religious belief that is *the condition for the possibility* of the theological virtue as well as to the theological virtue itself – unfortunate because, as we shall see

---

[14]   Though the Kierkegaardian warning is most apt just here: it is in the *application* of the distinction between flesh and spirit that we see contending mentalities at work.

[15]   The other two are hope and charity.

later, it leads to a confusion by which we transpose the proper intentionality of the virtue to its own condition as object.

This central image of 'covenant' perhaps explains why within Christian theology 'faith' is thought of *as* a virtue, since the trust and fidelity which together constitute it, can waver or grow strong as it is tested by harsh or easy conditions of life. Its centrality may also remind us of the ancient necessities of patriarchal political leadership – to inspire trust and command loyalty.

But this whole *mise en scène* of tribal life is an imaginative model both of what lies beyond 'the world' and of how the world appears from this point of transcendence.[16] My intention in saying this is not a dismissive or even reductive one, though we may well still recoil from or be unmoved by the metaphorics of patriarchy, covenant and redemption, with our implied responsibility through sin for the death of Jesus, though there may be non-oppressive versions of this.[17]

A different image is provided by Michelangelo's *Creation of Adam* in which there seems to be a reconciliation of the conflict between love and raw tyrannical power. As Peter Winch points out,[18] the picture shows love as the power to move the human heart by consent. But that the *Creation of Adam* is a *picture* of such power hardly implies that there is no such creative power.[19] The picture draws on our experience of love in the human realm, and although the orthodox move here is to stress that it only inadequately represents the *reality* of God's loving power, it nevertheless *perfectly* adequately serves its function, which is to represent an *idea* of loving power that transcends our human understanding, so that as our experience of the possibilities of love develops the picture is still there to represent it, like a kind of receding horizon at the edge of understanding: the image calls up a possibility which it represents, one whose gradual embodiment is projected back into our reading of the image. For those of us who are nostalgic former believers, the idea has a *regulative* function – but that is entirely consistent with the belief that it is *constitutive*.

[16] E.g., Isaiah 40:6–8: 'all flesh is grass . . . but the word of our God shall stand forever'.
[17] Perhaps the *Imitatio Christi* should not have been allowed to fall into the hands of the present writer in early adolescence.
[18] See Peter Winch, 'The Meaning of Religious Language' in *Trying to Make Sense* (Oxford: Basil Blackwell, 1987. pp. 74, 78–80).
[19] It is after all a classical claim that the scriptures are pictorial representations for the ignorant of the eternal truths of Neoplatonism.

ii. In order to look more closely now at the key distinctions surrounding religious belief and belief in God, it is convenient to
return to the newspaper commentaries that came after the
London bombings. One commentator was the philosopher
Jonathan Glover, who wrote about the possibilities of dialogue
with those who subscribe to the Islamist beliefs that were thought
to lie behind the bombings; in doing so he inevitably revealed his
own conception of 'religious belief':

> Different systems of belief, especially over religion, are often
> thought impossible to discuss. But the history of philosophy has
> been a sustained investigation into the difference between
> good reasons and bad reasons for holding beliefs. Teaching
> philosophy involves questioning people together. "You think
> this while she thinks that. Do either of you have reasons that
> should convince me that your view is the right one?" Notori-
> ously, philosophers disagree, so there is no set of "right"
> answers to learn from the teacher. Students end up with differ-
> ent beliefs. But if things go well they hold their final beliefs
> more tentatively, aware of how precarious the foundations of
> any beliefs are. In religious and ideological conflicts, this sense
> of precariousness is the antidote to fanaticism.[20]

'This sense of precariousness' is, *pace* Glover, hardly the antidote
to fanaticism – it is more likely to increase than diminish it. The
fanaticism he refers to is the expression of an intemperate mentality, and the antidote is *sophrosune*. There is a further intellectu-
alist bias in Glover's description of the process of dialogue. These
beliefs also structure a life-identity; for instance, within the Judeo-
Christian tradition a formation of subjectivity takes shape around
the scriptural psycho-drama into which the nascent believer is initi-
ated – indeed it is the psycho-drama that makes them into 'believers' at all, since to be a believer is to take up one's allotted role in
the drama played out between God and his people. The *role of
believer* is that of someone whose 'faith' in the sense of trust in
God's Word is *won*, and whose fidelity or 'faithfulness' in the sense
of submission to God's Law, is *demanded*. Hindu, Jain, Buddhist or
other East Asian practitioners are not 'believers' in this sense of a

---

[20] 'Dialogue is the only way to end this cycle of violence', *The Guardian* Wednesday July
27, 2005.

dramatic role within a turbulent *Heilsgeschichte*. But this is not to say that they have no religious beliefs.

iii. The problem with Glover's remarks is that 'religious' people even of the most temperate and least fanatical kind are likely to deny that the outcome of philosophical dialogue should be a *tentativeness of* belief that arises from realising their precarious foundations. They will wonder whether they are properly *tentative*, and whether they even *have* foundations.

Unfortunately there is confusion here and it resides in the failure to make significant distinctions. One main problem lies in the awkward ambiguity I have already mentioned of the expressions 'belief in God' and 'faith'; another lies in the cultural bias which assimilates both of these to 'religious belief'. In the psychodrama of the religions of the Book, 'belief in God' or 'faith' in the sense of trust and reciprocal fidelity can hardly be properly tentative – tentativeness here would simply be ambivalence. But, of course, Glover is no doubt *not* referring to this phenomenon at all. But what then is he referring to?

One standard assumption that philosophers make is that we can only rationally 'believe in God' in this attitudinal sense if we have good reason to believe that there is a God at all, and the standard verdict is that this existential belief that there is a God (the uncaused cause) is unproven or very precarious indeed in its foundations. Other philosophers, notably D.Z. Phillips, have pointed out how this procedure misunderstands the nature of the belief that there is a God and treats it as though it were akin to an empirical existential belief.[21] It is as though we had found a tribe who worshipped the Yeti and we were trying to convince them that there was no Yeti to worship by using the appropriate investigative tools for finding Yetis, a rare beast, but still a beast that can in principle be discovered by using those tools.

But, first, it is not obvious that the alleged 'proofs' constitute investigative tools at all, even if they were conceived as an independent route to establishing the rationality and truth of theism. Admittedly they are often taken to provide such rational underpinning, but while not everyone agrees that they do this wholly

---

[21] See, e.g., his 'At the Mercy of Method' in Timothy Tessin and Mario von der Ruhr (eds.), *Philosophy and the Grammar of Religious Belief* (Basingstoke: Macmillan, 1995), pp. 1–15.

inadequately, they seem more like an intellectual *reprise* of what they allegedly underpin than a genuine underpinning. This is not to say that they might not guide people towards a way of seeing the world that is conducive to the formation of religious belief. Secondly, and more importantly, it makes more sense to think, not in terms of the evidence for or against the *particular belief* that an existential proposition is true, but rather in terms of *belief formation* as it arises in relation to a whole system of propositions, in terms of 'theistic belief' rather than the belief that there is a God.

The standard objection need not take the dubious form of insisting that one should independently and *in advance* establish that there is a God to have confidence in. It may simply be a demand that believers (or, more to the point, someone on their behalf) should show that they have good reason to continue with their religious practices by securing the logically prior existential belief that there is a God. But this is the same misunderstanding, and the 'good reasons' for continuing with the religious practices are, for better or worse, internal to the system of belief.[22]

The standard assumption, then, itself is controversial. For many philosophers these are *basic* beliefs, themselves foundations, part of a noetic structure, to use a phrase of Plantinga's – there are neither good grounds for them, nor bad, not at least in the sense of further and more basic beliefs that serve as some kind of evidence in their favour. Some philosophers follow Plantinga here and claim that although they are basic, they are not arbitrary but *warranted*. But the same issue arises. Are we talking about the 'warrant' for believing that there is a God, or for the whole system of theistic belief? It is *tempting* to think of the existential belief as having a kind of warrant in experience, but it seems more likely to be an illusion generated by the prior presence of the *system* of belief. Thus one might, in the spirit of Sir Francis Bacon, declare that 'God never wrought miracle to convince atheism, because his ordinary works convince it'.[23] But such a sense of warrant relies on an already developed theological perspective. It is the work of the

---

[22] I can hardly not here acknowledge that this sounds like the notorious Wittgensteinian move that renders religion immune from any kind of criticism. But it only renders it immune from the wrong kind of criticism. It is not a strategy for protecting or defending religion, as we shall see.

[23] 'Of Atheism' in Francis Bacon, *The Essays* [1625], ed John Pitcher (Harmondsworth: Penguin, 1986).

imagination reflected back on itself – of course it is plain that the earth is the work of God's hand, as plain as that he has implanted in us the belief that he exists. By contrast, there seems no warrant at all for the *system* of theistic belief. There is no warrant for *any* particular formation of religious belief; it is rather the case that the instinctive sense of transcendence is what warrants our perception of *the world* as a limited whole.

iv. The phenomenology for a 'believer' is the immediacy and self-evidence in a particular cultural form of the apprehension of this transcendence. For a *believer* (and I use the term with the distinctive Abrahamic resonance) that apprehension takes the form of a particular dramatic narrative at a particular point in its literary and creative development as it meets crises of incomprehension in the face of terrible events. The object of 'theistic belief' is the *whole system of reference* – the narrative – within which the attitudes of 'faith' are embedded. It is the narrative that one comes to believe, or, better, to which one gives one's assent,[24] and the *imagination* is a crucial part of the process. It is the narrative that is basic. That there is a God is a proposition assent to which is implicit in assent to the narrative of his deeds. As Wittgenstein remarked in *On Certainty*, 'When we first begin to believe anything, what we believe is not a single proposition, it is a whole system of propositions. (Light dawns gradually over the whole).'[25] We are not seeking evidence for an existential belief but rational credentials for a complex that reprises the whole narrative, a God who ... And there seems no way of establishing that there *really is* such a God independently of conversion and 'acceptance-as-true', and that does not establish that it is 'really' true, either. This is not a 'fideist' claim, since 'faith' is embedded *within* the form of religious belief to which one gives one's assent: such assent is a leap of imagination, not of faith. Nor is it an 'anti-realist' claim. Those whose assent is compelled by the narrative implicitly believe that it is true that there is a God, that in giving their assent to the narrative they assent to a true even if not adequate representation of his nature and works, a qualification which gives us

[24] "This message (the Gospels) are seized on by men believingly (i.e. lovingly). *That* is the certainty characterising this particular acceptance-as-true, not something *else.*" (Wittgenstein, *Culture and Value* trans Peter Winch (Oxford: Basic Blackwell, 1980), p. 32e.
[25] Wittgenstein, *On Certainty* (Oxford: Basil Blackwell, 1969) § 141.

the terms of a distinction between naïve and critical realists.[26] But while such narrative visions of how things are need to be compelling, they are not as it were compulsory. To put it another way, what is primitive is a vision of the world that is capable of compelling assent, the immediate and self-evident apprehension of it as a limited and transcended whole. It is a compelling vision for those who are compelled, but it is not compulsory, as I have said. For many, but by no means most of us in the West these particular stories have lost their efficacy. But if we think in global terms they retain their potency, often in dangerous forms.

4. Towards the idea of a moral transcendence

However, this is not to say that the vision cannot be challenged or undermined by events. In our own age of human and natural catastrophe (*"What will happen to us now? We have done all God asked"*[27]) we may well recall Voltaire's reaction to the Lisbon earthquake of the eighteenth century. The logical point here, though, is not that an existential belief is *falsified* by the evidence of dreadful circumstances, but that a particular vision starts to unravel, loses its hold on the imagination – except that it is also *often* sustained even in the same dreadful circumstances.[28] Loss of *faith* in God's goodness may bring about the abandonment of the theistic form of religious belief which is its condition. It may take the form of the thought that there is after all no God, but this is in the same case as the affirmation that God really does exist, where 'really' serves merely as an emphatic. The believer will want to say that it is true that there is a God, and the non-believer that it is false, but these are endorsements of their belief or non-belief grounded in their faith or loss of faith. This is a corollary of the claim that the belief that there is a God is implicit in conversion or the dawning of assent to a whole system of belief. Nor does this conceptual limit mean that the believer and non-believer don't after all believe some proposition to be true or false. The point of

---

[26]   Indeed some of what pass for 'religious beliefs' are systematic meta-beliefs about the *status* of the narratives themselves, e.g. as a true and accurate record of the days of creation.

[27]   Said by a survivor of the recent earthquake in Kashmir.

[28]   Which sounds like 'death by a thousand qualifications', though there is no implication that *nothing* will count against the proposition that God loves us. Nevertheless the love of God becomes terrifyingly 'mysterious'.

talking about religious belief as a vision is that it is a *vision of how things are*. To say that the belief that there is a God cannot be independently verified does not imply that it cannot be independently true (or false), which is surely part of the point of an anti-verificationist realism here. That is our condition.

ii. I have referred to the capacity of forms of religious belief to compel assent or 'acceptance-as-true', to engage and inform the imagination, and wish here to resist a suggestion that these ungrounded beliefs are in some way the object of a *commitment* – a fallacy that I claimed earlier to derive from the conflation of 'faith' with 'religious belief'. Faith is a matter of commitment, 'religious belief' is not. Wittgenstein seems to make this mistake in *Culture and Value*:

> It strikes me that a religious belief could only be something like a passionate commitment to a system of reference. Hence, although it's *belief*, it's really a way of living, or a way of assessing life. (p. 64e)

The first sentence seems to me to be a significant intellectual error: we commit ourselves to a course of action or a project, to repeated acts of trust and fidelity, for instance, in the circumstances which demand them, and that is why we tend to associate 'faith' and 'commitment'. But religious belief is not a *project* – or, better, it provides the terms (which we assent to) within which these projects for our commitment are conceived. Perhaps the source of the error lies in the difficulty of conceiving the intellectual alternatives when we dismiss traditional natural theology as an underpinning to theistic belief, and when religious belief is anyway starting to lose its hold. If we cannot know these things, cannot rationally justify them, then perhaps, we think, they are something we commit ourselves to, as an existential choice. But even our existential choices are laid out for us in the sense that they present themselves within the parameters of our world picture. The language that belongs quite properly to the theological virtue of *faith*, which is a language of longing and striving and commitment, including for some a longing for certainty, is here simply transferred and applied to the terms in which that faith is expressed. But these terms compel *acceptance* not commitment. The point is that one does not have a passionate commitment *to* a 'system of reference': it is rather that systems of reference determine what one *could* have a passionate commitment towards. The relation of the believer to the system of reference is one of 'acceptance-as-true'. The commitment is not to the system but to something like the *recollection and recalling* of the system, in the sense of a keeping it present in a spirit of mindfulness and fidelity that is inspired by its content. This is a possible object of commitment, a kind of *keeping faith* ('keep the truth which thou hast found').

Indeed this commitment to its lively recollection seems to be the proper disposition towards a religious belief. Wittgenstein's remark – 'Hence, although it's *belief*, it's really a way of living, or a way of assessing life' – applies well to belief in the Last Judgment. Recollection of the *dies irae . . . quando judex est venturus* is supposed to admonish and concentrate the mind in daily life and not just at Requiems. Its acceptance-as-true is one way in which someone might be summoned to a sense of moral seriousness, though we may quibble over its content. Its regulative role does not rule out its status as a religious belief. In his famous discussion[29] Wittgenstein does not claim that it is has a *merely* regulative role: he simply insists that it *has* such a role and then points out the strange logic of religious as opposed, say, to empirical belief. There is nothing reductive in that. Johannes Climacus[30] would call it a 'subjectively appropriated' belief.

iii. We can easily enough imagine, not to say find, non-theistic cultures in which the dramatic role of the 'believer' is not in the repertoire. There are also 'seekers', 'renouncers', 'disciples', and 'followers of the Way'. Others think of themselves as 'practitioners' rather than 'believers'.

This is not to deny that there are overlaps and correspondences. Confidence (*sraddha*) in the Buddha, as one who is able to show the way, is said to increase as the way unfolds. Under the pressure of his existential crisis, Siddhartha seizes on the sight of the mendicant as an image of liberation, which then has to be tested and explored. 'Dharma farers' seek a way that takes them from their erratic wandering in the jungle of *samsara* to liberation and release, insight and compassion. The jungle and the desert are different but equally oppressive terrains, and finding the

---

[29]   See Wittgenstein, Lectures and Conversations on Aesthetics, Psychology & Religious Belief, ed Cyril Barrett (Oxford: Basil Blackwell, 1966), pp. 52–71.
[30]   The pseudonymous author of *Concluding Unscientific Postscript.*

safety of the village clearing[31] is a more modest metaphorical aim than finding the Promised Land, but it is the *application* of these metaphors that counts. Both may serve as images of our interior condition, though the journey through the desert is something that happens to a *people* and the wandering in the jungle something that happens to an *individual*. But it is significant that the Buddha addresses his sermons to his *bhikkhus* as a community, striving to free themselves from the greed, hatred and delusion that also infects their *experience* of community; – and that St Paul's discussion of the gifts of the flesh and the gifts of the spirit addresses how a community of believers in the saving power of Christ *ought to live*.

iv. Even though Buddhists tend to discount theism on the grounds of its indeterminability, which is fine for those who are not yet or no longer compelled by that narrative vision of a saving power, there is an analogous disjunction within Buddhism between possible experience and what lies beyond it – *karma* following us over many life times, countless aeons spent wandering in the rounds of existence. These claims are just as indeterminable as theistic belief, and no more nor less independently true or false, though this is hardly a compelling reason to give them one's assent. On the other hand, there is an experiential residue, both for non-traditional Buddhists and for the post-religious more generally. This is what I wish to call moral transcendence, release, if there is any such (a matter of *hope*, this, rather than 'faith'), from the Cave of the egocentric or communal predicament, the point of departure for which is the discovery of the mechanisms that are the condition of that predicament.

The quest for such a residue is plainly seen in the work of such writers as Matthew Arnold, Richard Braithwaite and Don Cupitt, as well as in such movements as the Sea of Faith and non-traditional forms of Western Buddhism. The potential error for such movements, however, lies in their temptation towards *anti-realism*. Finding a moral and experiential residue, an independent, interior discourse about the alleged realities of love and courage, for instance, is not the same as attempting a *reduction* of religious claims to claims about possible forms of experience. It is

---

[31] I am grateful to Christopher Bartley for pointing out these connotations of the term *samsara*.

predicated upon the loss of religious belief and upon the impos-
sibility, therefore, of faith in God. It is a matter of what truths can
be found in the midst of those ruins, truths which give the lie to
Kureishi's dismissal of religions without significant content or
force. But that is the wrong metaphor for seeking the truth. A
more apt one for where Truth stands is Donne's huge hill: 'and he
that will/Reach her, about must, and about must goe' . . .

6

THE VARIETIES OF NON-RELIGIOUS EXPERIENCE

Richard Norman

Are atheists missing something important? If theism does 'make a difference to the flow and perceived significance of someone's life', is it a difference which leaves the atheist at a disadvantage? The claim that secular humanists are indeed missing something could take two forms – either that the atheist's experience is *incomplete* or that it is *opaque*. The incompleteness claim I shall to some extent concede. There are indeed kinds of experience which theists can have – or at any rate could be having if their beliefs were true – but from which the atheist is debarred. I shall argue, however, that these are only particular and limited aspects of the five fundamental dimensions of human experience which I am going to discuss. The essential core of those five kinds of experience is as available to the atheist as to the theist. Without the core experiences our lives would indeed be diminished and impoverished, but just because they are essentially human, they are experiences in which we can all share. The aspects which are exclusively theistic, on the other hand, may well be kinds of experience which it would be good to have, but they are ones which we can live without. I do not have a precise criterion for distinguishing between experiences which it would be *good to have* – ones which theists think they have and atheists cannot have – and experiences which are *integral components of human life*. I hope however that my discussion of the particular examples will show the distinction to be a plausible one.

The *opacity* claim would be that though human beings do characteristically have the important kinds of experience which I have listed and will discuss, the atheist fails to understand the essentially religious nature of such experiences. The claim thus takes the form of a transcendental argument: that the possibility of such experiences presupposes the existence of a god or gods. I shall aim to show that any such transcendental argument is unsound. These essential human experiences are just that – forms of *human* experience, integral features of human life, aspects of what it is to be human. We do not need belief in a god in order to make sense of them or to explain their possibility.

The authority of the moral 'ought'

The first suggestion which I want to consider is that we have a distinctive experience of the authoritative character of moral values or moral judgements, and that theism makes best sense of this experience. Though I am not happy with the idea of a sharp divide between moral demands and other kinds of normative reasons, I accept that there is something to be explained here: the sense that we have of something which we ought or ought not to do, regardless of our own wants and inclinations. A theistic transcendental argument may then take the following form. The authority of morality, it may be said, is explicable only as a personal authority, since only persons can make claims on us of a kind which limit or override our own wants and inclinations. The force of moral demands cannot, however, be explained in terms of the claims which finite persons (such as other human beings) make on us; it can only be explained by the authority of a personal god.[1]

My reply to such an argument would be that the authority of the moral 'ought' *can* in fact be sufficiently explained in terms of the limits imposed on our actions by the recognition of other finite persons. The wrong that we do, when we do what morally we ought not to do, is always a wrong done to another person (normally another human being, but perhaps also a non-human animal). To make this reply sufficiently convincing I want to emphasise that when I refer to 'a wrong done to another person', I am not proposing a consequentialist or utilitarian account, in which the wrong perpetrated when, for instance, I tell a lie, or break a promise, is an independently identifiable harm of a generic kind. The position I am taking cuts across the traditional consequentialist/deontological divide. On the one hand, what is wrong about telling a lie is not the violation of some abstract

---

[1]   Cf. H. P. Owen, 'Why morality implies the existence of God', in *Philosophy of Religion*, ed. Brian Davies (Oxford: Oxford University Press, 2000).

free-floating 'duty'. The wrong is the wrong done *to the person to whom the lie is told.* On the other hand the consequentialist account is unsatisfactory because it fails to recognise the diversity of ways in which we can wrong others, which cannot all be subsumed under a general heading of causing suffering or pain or depriving others of possible happiness or well-being. If I lie to someone, the wrong I do to him is that of deceiving him. If I break my promise to someone, the wrong I do to her is the wrong of letting her down. If I treat someone unjustly or unfairly, the wrong I do to him may be the wrong of exploiting him. If I am ungrateful to someone, the wrong I do may be that of taking her for granted. If I coerce someone, the wrong I do may be that of violating his autonomy, of appropriating his life and treating him as a mere object. And so on.

Why might this be thought not to be a satisfactory account of the authority of the moral 'ought'? Here is one suggestion. Robert Adams, in the context of his defence of a 'modified divine command theory', says:

In all sin there is offense against a person (God), even when there is no offense against any other human person – for instance, if I have a vice which harms me but does not importantly harm any other human being. Therefore in the Judaeo-Christian tradition reactions which are appropriate when one has offended another person are felt to be appropriate reactions to any ethical fault, regardless of whether another human being has been offended.[2]

The case of moral wrongs which harm only oneself is the only problematic instance which he mentions. We might respond simply by rejecting the idea of moral duties to oneself – it is, after all, a contentious element in our moral thinking, rather than an integral component of the very idea of morality. Alternatively, if we do want to make sense of the idea, then we shall have to provide some account of how one can morally stand towards oneself as though towards another person – perhaps in terms of a relation of one part of the self to another and better part of oneself. I do not

[2] R. M. Adams, 'A Modified Divine Command Theory of Ethical Wrongness', in *Philosophy of Religion: An Anthology*, ed. C. Taliaferro and P. J. Griffiths (Oxford: Blackwell, 2003), p. 466.

know whether this can be done, but I do think that the idea of moral duties to oneself must stand or fall with the success or failure of such an attempt. Certainly we do not solve the problem by bringing in God, for if we explain moral duties to oneself by saying that they are indeed duties to another person, namely duties to God, then they are not after all duties to oneself, and we have lost precisely what we were supposed to be explaining.

The same response can be made to another argument attempting to show that moral concern cannot be explained simply as a concern for other human persons. Gordon Graham argues that we are committed to an 'absolute conception' of morality, the idea that moral considerations are *overriding*.[3] He takes this to entail that some kinds of action are unconditionally ruled out, whatever the circumstances, and he offers the example of slavery as something which would be generally regarded as absolutely wrong (p. 96). He then acknowledges that there is a problem as to how such a conception can be motivating and can be rational, if it requires us to act in certain ways even in circumstances where this may lead to a worse outcome. In response, he offers a 'transcendental argument' for what he calls 'moral faith' – the faith that acting morally 'is in my interests even when I do not and cannot know this', and that it 'will not ultimately conflict with personal or social well-being, appearances to the contrary notwithstanding' (p. 93).

> There is at least one absolute evil. Therefore we must make our conception of practical reason accord with its possibility. To do this we must presuppose that the conditions of its possibility prevail, and that to abhor this evil is better for us as agents and for the world in general than to accommodate it. We can only reasonably suppose this, however, if we hold that there exists some sort of Providence which makes the maintenance of these conditions its purpose. To believe coherently in the existence of absolute evil therefore requires us to believe in a providential God. (p. 96)

In reply I would want first to distinguish different senses in which moral requirements are 'overriding'. There is first the idea that moral requirements are binding 'irrespective of inclination'

3 Gordon Graham, *Evil and Christian Ethics* (Cambridge: Cambridge University Press, 2001), pp. 75–8.

(Graham p. 78) and do not derive their force from the desires and purposes which as individuals we may happen to have. This aspect of morality we can perfectly well account for in terms of the constraints imposed on our actions by other persons. That can also generate a stronger notion of overridingness – that morality is not just a matter of the promotion of well-being. A respect for other people's agency, for their autonomy or their rights, may support a strong conception of moral side-constraints, the recognition that certain ways of treating other human beings are ruled out, even though the acceptance of those constraints may lead to less well-being or to greater suffering. Promoting other's well-being, and preventing others' suffering, may not be the only requirements of moral concern and respect for others. We can account for these two senses in which moral requirements are overriding without necessarily having to make a third and still stronger claim – that morality 'absolutely' rules out certain kinds of actions, in any conceivable circumstances. Should we accept that stronger claim? I do not know. I do not see how we can rule out the possibility of some extreme emergency, in which it might be necessary for one group of human beings, for instance, to enslave another in order to prevent total disaster such as the complete destruction of all human life. Suppose, however, we do accept that some moral requirements are overriding in this strongest, 'absolute' sense. If we do, then such a conception is *not* supported by Graham's notion of moral faith, that God will ensure that acting morally is not ultimately in conflict with humans' personal and social well-being. For to make such a move is precisely to reject the very conception of morality which it was supposed to support – that morally requirements are binding in a way which can override the desire to promote human well-being. As with Adams' move, so with Graham's – by re-interpreting moral requirements as duties owed to God, or as duties underpinned by God's guarantees of our well-being, we eliminate precisely those distinctive features of morality which we were supposed to be trying to explain.

The experience of beauty

I turn now to the suggestion that the experience of beauty, in art and in nature, has an implicitly religious character. Here is one formulation of that idea, by John Haldane, who claims that 'the experience of the aesthetic may warrant religious beliefs' and that

this idea 'stand[s] in opposition to a common humanistic conception of art and the aesthetic as alternative sources of inspiration,
consolation and sustenance for those for whom theism is
unbelievable.'

> First, then, it is a familiar thought that natural beauty may offer
> an intimation of creation. Indeed, for many people now
> detached from traditional religious creeds and practices, the
> experience of nature may provide the best prospect of any
> sense of transcendence. . . . A second point of relevance . . . is
> that the aesthetic experience of nature has often provided
> inspiration for the making of works expressing attitudes of
> 'natural religion'. . . . [T]here is the sense of awe at the very
> being of the world. . . . There is also the sense of manifest
> design felt in observing the beauty of organisms whose parts
> stand in a fitting relation to one another and to the life of the
> whole. . . . A third consideration is that just as the experience of
> nature has led some to a belief in God, so has the experience of
> art: both art in general, as testifying again to the significance
> of beauty, and religious art in particular, as presenting aspects
> of the transcendent.[4]

That last sentence alludes to a special point about the experience
of religious art to which I will turn in a moment. I shall also say
something later about the invoking of the idea of 'transcendence'.
But what about the general claim, that the experience of beauty is
an intimation of experience of the divine? In contrast to the case
of morality, I find it difficult to locate any substantial argument
here. Haldane alludes to the argument from design, but I do not
see that the experience of beauty in the natural world adds any
independent weight to that argument. We may argue that the
intricate structure of a living organism, in which the different
parts interact with one another to serve the functions of the
whole, is evidence of a divine creator. We may also take delight in
the beauty of such structures. But if the design argument in the
end fails, as for standard reasons I think it does, the experience
of beauty cannot shore it up. The experience itself of course
remains, but we should accept it for what it is. I want to resist the

---

[4] John Haldane, *An Intelligent Person's Guide to Religion* (London: Duckworth, 2003),
pp. 151–5.

tendency of some theists to co-opt any experience of mystery and awe and claim it as an experience of the divine. 'Everything is what it is, and not another thing.' We can indeed be transported by experiences of beauty of all kinds, which lift us out of the routine of everyday life and can sustain and inspire us. That is a deep fact about human beings, but we should accept it as such and not try to turn it into something else. What is particularly unsatisfactory about the co-option of the experience of beauty by religious creeds is that, so far from accepting the mystery, it may seek to dispel it. The mystery of aesthetic delight is just that – mysterious – and to attempt to pin it down by interpreting it as an awareness of divine design is to threaten to undermine it by over-interpretation.

Haldane does however pose a genuine problem for the atheist when he turns to the specific case of religious art, and I want to consider this in more detail. He argues that any serious work of art is 'a presentation of the reality and values in which the work seeks to participate', and that in evaluating the work 'we are judging the credibility of what it proclaims' (pp. 171–2). It would seem to follow that if a work presents religious beliefs and values, the atheist is bound to reject those beliefs and values and is therefore committed to judging the work less highly. And this appears to exclude the atheist from fully appreciating and valuing religious works of art. One of Haldane's examples is Piero della Francesca's painting *The Resurrection* in Borgo San Sepolcro. The atheist might try to take refuge in praise of the formal qualities of the work, but as Haldane rightly says, its form and content are inseparable. The arrangement of the figures, with the sleeping soldiers in their poses of disarray 'contrasting with the simple sweeping contour of Christ', who divides the background landscape between the deadness of winter and the new life of spring – all of this serves to point up the content of the painting, and the painting seems to be inescapably religious (pp. 168–9).

I agree with Haldane that, like all Piero della Francesca's work, it is one of the supreme achievements of art. But, as an atheist, can I consistently say this? Haldane's argument could be set out formally as follows.

(1) 'A serious favourable appreciation of the aesthetic value of a work of art carries an implication of the acceptance of its content as constituting a consideration in favour of what is presented.' (p. 172)

(2) Atheists are precluded from accepting the content of a work of religious art as constituting a consideration in favour of what is presented.

(3) Therefore atheists are, to that extent, precluded from favourably appreciating the aesthetic value of religious art.

I accept premise (1). It is contentious, and I am not going to open up the matters for contention, but I agree that at least the finest works of art convey truths about our world and our experience, that they provide support for the truths which they convey, and that their doing so is an important part of their value. My quarrel is not with this, but with premise (2). The assumption here is that the truth presented by a religious work of art must itself be a religious truth. That is what I want to question. Of course Piero's painting is a depiction of the resurrection, but it does not give us any reason for believing the claim that Jesus rose from the dead. How could it do so? (It's not as though it were photographic evidence or anything of that sort.) The truths which it conveys are human truths, truths which help us in the understanding of our human condition. Like any great work of art, it conveys such truths by drawing on our own experience and helping us to see a significance in that experience. It says something about the ability of human beings to rise above suffering. And that is specifically a truth about human beings, because the features of the work which convey it are the recognisable human characteristics of the figure rising from the tomb. Typically of Piero, there is a deeply enigmatic quality in the figure, but also a profound stillness, a nobility and a serenity which speaks of suffering overcome through contemplation and understanding. The qualities apparent in the risen Jesus are similar to those of the figures in the right-hand side of Piero's *The Flagellation*, another meditation on suffering and the human response to suffering.

The truths conveyed by *The Resurrection* are also to be found in the figures of the sleeping soldiers at the base of the tomb. Again the truths are conveyed in the significance of the poses and expressions of the human figures. They say something about the propensity of human beings to miss the miracles that are going on in the world around us – in this case, to be oblivious to the transformation and renewal of human life, and to the corresponding transformation and renewal of the natural world, as represented by the change from the bare trees on the left of the picture to the new growth on the right. In these ways, then, the content of

the picture provides 'considerations in favour of what is presented', and these considerations are as accessible for the atheist
as for the theist. The general point is that the truths conveyed by
great religious works of art are human truths. And that is because
religious iconography is powerful and compelling when it draws
on shared human experience and works to enhance our understanding of that experience.

The experience of meaningful narratives

It is sometimes suggested that without religion we would be bereft
of the stories which enrich our lives. In the Christian tradition the
relevant stories would be primarily those in the Bible, from the
creation story, the Garden of Eden, Noah and the flood, Abraham
and Isaac, and so on, through to the Gospel narratives and also
including the parables in the Gospels. Some of these stories, in
particular the Incarnation, Crucifixion, and Resurrection, also of
course have the status of doctrines, but it is their distinctive role as
stories, along with the others in the list, that I want to consider.
What is special about stories, I take it, is their enactment of
important human experiences as they occur in the lives of individuals, and drawing on these can help us to shape our own lives,
help us to recognise features of them as exemplifying a universal
pattern and thus to make sense of them. The stories of anger and
strife and reconciliation, of fear and courage, of love and betrayal
and loyalty, of death and despair and new hope, because they are
presented as the lived experiences of individuals, bring home to
us what these things mean in concrete and particular terms.

It is significant that every religious tradition has its repertoire of
stories, of archetypal experiences enacted in the lives of individuals. But if we are considering them not as literal truths but as
stories, meaningful fictions which shape our experience, then
they are not confined to religions. Every culture has a wealth of
stories – myths and sagas, the great epic poems inherited from
oral traditions, fairy stories and fables, novels and plays, through
to popular fiction and in the modern world the stories offered in
profusion by films, television plays and the 'soaps'. The length of
the list confirms the ubiquity and depth of the need. By the same
token, however, it confirms that religions and their stories are by
no means the only source for meeting the need. And if religious

stories themselves perform this role as *stories*, as meaningful fictions, they are in that capacity as available to the atheist as to the theist.

Still, it may be said, we have to discriminate. This abundance of stories is all very well, but not just any stories will do, we need the *right* stories. I agree, and when we think of the distorting stereotypes offered by so much popular fiction, in both printed and visual media, we can recognise the importance of getting the story right. But we are talking about the truth appropriate to fictions here, the truth of fictions which honestly capture the reality and complexity of human experience. In that sense we may well judge that, compared with contemporary stories which glamorise power and wealth and violence, stories such as that of a child born in an outhouse to lowly parents and visited by shepherds are preferable – but they can be preferred without being tied to a context of theistic belief.

Some religious traditions, however, including orthodox Christianity, would claim to have 'the right story' in a stronger sense. They would claim to be able to provide an overarching narrative which makes sense of 'the broad sweep of history'.[5] Here I refer to Haldane again. Against the postmodernists, he says, he sides with the modernists and pre-modernists who see the need for so-called 'meta-narratives, overarching accounts of events that subsume other more local narratives' and which locate the 'diversity of cultural forms and life-styles . . . within a larger picture which gives it a meaning.' For Haldane that larger picture is the Christian meta-narrative, the view of human history as a struggle between good and evil and as the working out of a divine plan, beginning with the Creation and the Fall and leading to some eventual consummation. This, he says, is a narrative which can reconcile the pessimists' acknowledgement of the darker aspects of human history with the need to see in that history a direction which can be a source of hope. He notes that not only the secular grand narratives but also the postmodernists themselves fall back on some form of progressivism (112–3). He suggests however that the need to view human history teleologically, as having a direction and moving towards a goal, cannot be met without a belief in divine agency.

---

[5]   Ibid. p. 97.

It is doubtful . . . whether anything short of real purposeful agency can provide history with a teleology. If that is right, and if the idea of a meta-narrative has rational appeal, then so should the notion that ultimately the course of human history is a religious one, a movement towards or away from God. (p. 122)

As the risk of sounding postmodernist, I have doubts about the need for grand narratives. The idea seems to conflate two different things, the needs for 'stories' in the strict sense, as concrete and particular enactments of aspects of human life which enable us to give them a practical significance, and the need for an objective and literal understanding of the broad features of human history and the human condition. Both are needed, but the latter will not appropriately take the form of an overarching story. Insofar as we need stories, we need them in their diversity, to do justice to the nuances of our experiences and their felt particularity. They cannot all be subsumed into a single story which gives a unique meaning to human history.

Secular humanism has itself been criticised as offering a naïve progressivism, a faith in the onward march of humanity towards an inevitable future from which irrationality and superstition will have vanished. That particular 'grand narrative' is difficult to sustain, especially in the light of the past century's manifestations of the darker side of human behaviour, and to that extent the hopes of the Enlightenment have become tarnished. But if that simplistic progressivism is not available, it does not follow that we have to fall back on a religious teleology in order to sustain our hopes and give meaning to our activities. What we do need, it is true, is some sense of our lives as part of a larger picture, having a meaningful continuity both with the past and with the future. If what will happen after our own deaths does not matter to us, if we have no sense of inheriting things of value from our predecessors and bequeathing them to future generations, then it is difficult to see how what we do with our lives can have any deep significance for us. That necessary sense of continuity across generations can to some extent be fostered by the appropriate stories – novels or plays or films which present the pattern of a whole life, or the lives of successive generations, or which shows characters wrestling with contested understandings of their past and their relationship to the previous generation. But the sense of continuity is also of course rooted in our direct experience, of family relationships,

and of ties to a wider community, local or national or international, cultural or political.

To sustain our hopes, and to understand our activities as having
a point, we need not only a sense of continuity, but also a recognition of the possibilities of change. We do not, I think, need any
fiction about the inevitability of progress, or a meta-narrative
about the onward march of humanity, or the mission of this or
that country to bring freedom, democracy and fast food to the rest
of the world, but it is difficult to see how we could maintain much
of a commitment to a whole range of human activities unless we
had at least realistic hopes in the possibility of progress. For that,
however, we need not a meta-narrative but strictly empirical
grounds for guarded optimism. Those grounds are, I should say,
available. It seems to me undeniable, for instance, that the lives of
the great majority of people in this country are substantially better
than were the lives of the great majority a century ago, and that
this change for the better has come about as a result of the
conscious and committed endeavours of countless men and
women to achieve it. Clearly this is not the place to argue the
point. Here I maintain only that the basis for hope, and thus for
the possibility of meaningful activity, does not depend on any
meta-narrative which sees our lives as part of a divine plan.

The experience of transcendence

It is sometimes said that atheistic humanism cannot be fully satis-
fying because it cannot meet the need for the experience of
transcendence. It is quite unclear what this means, and though
the accusation is regularly made I doubt whether there is any one
point which it consistently identifies. Sometimes the word 'transcendence' is used in the same vague way as talk of 'spirituality',
with the implication that a life without theistic belief is condemned to be shallow and superficial. Perhaps the implication is
that atheistic humanism precludes those transfiguring moments
which lift us above the humdrum level of everyday life, or that it
offers nothing to aim at beyond the pursuit of physical well-being
and material goods. Such suggestions are certainly made, but I
take them to be too obviously false to merit serious discussion.

Talk of 'transcendence' also draws on the more specifically
philosophical, metaphysical sense of the word, with its reference

to a possible non-natural world which lies beyond sense-experience. It is true that many versions of theism, including the dominant strand in Christianity, have been tied to a broadly Platonic metaphysics, but to suggest that this points to a lack in atheistic humanism is plainly question-begging. There may or may not be a rational case to be made for the existence of a transcendent realm, but short of such a case, we cannot say that there is a human *need* to hold such beliefs.

There may however be a genuine point to be made by talk of a need for the experience of transcendence, and the best sense that I can make of it is this: that human beings need the experience of the non-human. Without such experience, it may be said, the human world is too limited, too shut in on itself, too cosy. We need a relationship to 'the Other', and that means not just other human beings. We can understand our own humanity only through a relationship to a non-human world.

I think there is something in this, but the source from which such a need is met is most obviously our relationship to the *natural* world rather than to any non-natural realm. There are many dimensions to our experience of nature, and I have already said something about the experience of beauty in nature, but another dimension is certainly the experience of a relationship to something larger than the human world, which in that sense 'transcends' our merely human concerns and puts them into perspective. It can come from the awareness of other living things as having a life of their own, alien and separate and mysterious. Still more strongly is the encounter with the non-human to be found in our experience of the inanimate natural world, and a locus classicus here of course is Wordsworth. Recalling in Book I of *The Prelude* the incident when as a boy he had rowed out onto the moonlit lake and seen the 'huge cliff' rearing up, he says:

. . . and after I had seen
That spectacle, for many days, my brain
Work'd with a dim and undetermin'd sense
Of unknown modes of being; in my thoughts
There was a darkness, call it solitude,
Or blank desertion, no familiar shapes
Of hourly objects, images of trees,
Of sea or sky, no colours of green fields;
But huge and mighty Forms that do not live

Like living men mov'd slowly through my mind
By day and were the trouble of my dreams.[6]

It is the alien and inhuman character of these 'unknown modes of
being' that makes them troubling, but for Wordsworth, especially
in retrospect, the experience is not just a negative one. By reveal-
ing a world beyond the merely human, it is also uplifting. Wordsworth immediately goes on to speak of how 'the passions that
build up our human soul' are sustained . . .

Not with the mean and vulgar works of Man,
But with high objects, with enduring things,
With life and nature, purifying thus
The elements of feeling and of thought,
And sanctifying, by such discipline,
Both pain and fear, until we recognize
A grandeur in the beatings of the heart.
(435–441)

We can find in this passage, then, an expression of the idea that
our human lives need this encounter with the non-human, that
such experience puts us in our place and reminds us of our
limited importance within a larger universe, and that it can be fed
by our relationship to the natural world and does not require any
sense of the supernatural or the divine. But in using Wordsworth
thus, I have cheated. The passage which I have just quoted is
introduced with these lines:

Wisdom and Spirit of the universe!
Thou Soul that art the Eternity of Thought!
That giv'st to forms and images a breath
And everlasting motion! not in vain,
By day or star-light thus from my first dawn
Of Childhood didst Thou intertwine for me
The passions that build up our human Soul . . .
(428–434)

Here Wordsworth, looking back on his childhood experience,
succumbs to the appeal of the idea that if nature has this capacity

6   William Wordsworth, *The Prelude*, 1805 text, ed. E. de Selincourt (London: Oxford
University Press, 1960), Book I, lines 417–427.

to ennoble human passions, this must point to some pre-established harmony between the natural and the human world, to the presence of the same 'spirit' or 'soul' in nature and in the human frame. In these lines the idea is formulated in the language of pantheism, and for Wordsworth himself that pantheism was increasingly transmuted into the espousal of orthodox Christianity. I see no need to follow Wordsworth down that road. On the contrary, putting it into a theistic framework seems to me, if anything, to negate the original insight. It is precisely the non-human separateness of nature that sustains and nourishes us. To suppose that nature can do this for us because it too is the embodiment of qualities of wisdom and intelligence, of a spirit which has a knowledge of and concern for our own human lives, is ironically to anthropomorphise nature and thereby diminish the experience. The encounter with the non-human is essentially an experience of something alien and indifferent, that is what is important about it, and the atheistic rendering of the experience captures this more accurately than the theistic version.

The experience of vulnerability and fragility

The last form of experience in my list, the experience of fragility, is different from the others. The claim to be considered here is not that the experience of fragility is itself a valuable and essential form of human experience. Rather, the suggestion may be that by accepting the fact of human fragility, by honestly acknowledging it and coming to terms with it, we may be given an intimation of the truth of a religious perspective and may come to see how it can give a meaning to our lives. And the further implication may be that the atheist humanist, wedded perforce to the Promethean assumption that human beings can forge a meaning for their lives from their limited human resources and their own strength of will, are both condemned to futility and debarred from the insights which an acceptance of our fragility can bring.

The acknowledgement of human frailty is a theme explored by John Cottingham. He speaks of 'the sense of possible failure and futility that haunts our quest for meaning', and draws attention to the ways in which our projects may succeed or fail for reasons over

which we have no control.[7] Cottingham's response to the fact of
our fragility then seems to oscillate between two courses. On the
one hand there is the idea that we can come to terms with our
vulnerability by what he calls 'some kind of radical interior modification' (p. 79), honestly accepting our dependence, adjusting
our values to it and recognising what really matters. But there is
also the idea that if our lives are not to be futile, we need some
kind of external guarantee, the reassurance of what he refers to as
'the resilience of goodness', and that seems in the end to require
a belief that the things over which we have no control are nevertheless guided by a divine power working for good.

The 'radical interior modification' is something which Cottingham sees as essentially religious, something which he equates with
the 'spirituality' which 'the great religions have typically aimed to
achieve' (p. 79). He also refers to it as

> the insight that through giving up our attachment to the trap-
> pings of success, position, money, we become more fully
> human – more open to the plight of those around us with
> whom, despite our surface differences, we share so much; such
> a transformation brings us closer to realising how to live in a
> world where, sooner or later, we will have to give up everything
> – our youth, our health, many of those we love, and in the end,
> even our lives. Status and power temporarily insulate us from
> our inherent human vulnerability; but in plumbing the depths
> of that vulnerability we discover what truly matters. (p. 76)

I do not see this insight as a specifically religious one, but as one
fully accessible from a secular perspective. In coming to terms
with the vicissitudes of life we can, all of us, come to recognise the
superficiality of wealth and fame and power and understand what
really matters.

But this line of thought also has its limits. It is one thing to talk of
'giving up our attachment to the trappings of success, position,
money'. It would be quite another thing to say that our vulnerability
to bereavement and loss should lead us to give up our attachment
to those we love. The interior modification can only take us so far,
it cannot insulate us against grief or loss – or if it did, it would only
be by hardening us and deadening our feelings. Perhaps that is why

---

[7]   John Cottingham, *On the Meaning of Life* (London: Routledge, 2003), p. 67.

Cottingham's argument seems to move from the need for interior modification to the need for exterior consolation. What I take him to be saying, in fact, is that the interior modification can itself generate an insight into the truth of the relevant belief about an external reality. He acknowledges the difficulties which stand in the way of an acceptance of religious beliefs. Initially, then, he plays down the need for the beliefs. He stresses the importance 'not of doctrines but of *practices*: techniques of meditation and prayer, techniques for self-examination and greater self-awareness' (pp. 87–8). In response to the suggestion that the practices presuppose belief he suggests that 'belief, in the sense of subscribing to a set of theological propositions, is not in fact central to what it is to be religious' (p. 88). In due course, however, he moves to what I take to be a rather different suggestion – that by engaging in the practices we can get 'intimations' of the truth of the beliefs.

What Cottingham appears to propose at this point is a distinctive form of transcendental argument. Drawing on Pascal, he suggests that by engaging in the 'spiritual practices' which embody the religious attitude to life, we may gain insight into the truth of the corresponding beliefs. His example is that of saying grace before meals – a practice which turns the meeting of a mere physical need into an acknowledgement of our finitude and dependence and our place in a larger whole. He suggests that

> . . . the illuminations that come from the practice of spirituality cannot be accessed by means of rational argument alone, since the relevant experiences are not available to us during those times when we are adopting the stance of detached rationality. . . . [O]ur human awareness . . . indisputably includes experiences in which spiritual values are made manifest – experiences in which, arguably, we have intimations of a transcendent world of meaning . . . (p. 100)

The important claim here seems to be that there are experiences which presuppose the truth of certain beliefs, but that if we start by trying to deciding rationally whether those beliefs are true, we shall cut ourselves off from the experiences. If, however, we open ourselves up to the experiences, and act as though the beliefs were true, we shall come to see that they are indeed true.

There are cases which fit that description. Sometimes, for instance, it is only by trusting someone, by making that leap of faith, that you can establish a relationship of mutual confidence and thereby come to see that the other person can indeed be trusted. Or again, it may be that only in loving someone can we become fully aware of what is lovable about them. In such cases the active commitment brings about a Gestalt switch which enables us to see more clearly the truth on which the commitment depends.

The difficulty for such a position, however, is that we have to be able to distinguish between two kinds of case:

(a) S acts as though p were true and thereby comes to believe p, where this is a case of self-deception or unthinking habit, inducing a belief which remains ungrounded.

(b) S acts as though p were true and thereby comes to see what it is that makes p true.

In cases such as that of grace before meals giving us 'intimations of meaning', we need some reason for thinking that they are cases of kind (b) rather than kind (a). In my examples of trust and of love, there is at any rate something that the person can say about what makes p true – what makes the other lovable, how she knows that he is trustworthy. Admittedly, the point of the 'Gestalt switch' account is that what makes p true is more difficult to recognise for someone who has not made the commitment. Still, there has to be *something* which S can say, and which can convey to others what it is that grounds the commitment. Think of the duck-rabbit. Someone who cannot see it as a duck can be told 'Look, that's the beak.' They will not be able to see it as a beak unless they have made the switch to seeing the figure as a picture of a duck; nevertheless, saying to them 'That's the beak' can help them to make the switch. But in the case of the religious believer, if the belief is induced by the practice, and if there is *nothing* that he can say about what it is that he is now aware of which supports his belief, then his position is indistinguishable from that of the self-deceiver in cases of kind (a). Rather than being like that of the person whose love makes them more aware of what is lovable in the other person, it is like that of someone who thinks, perhaps unconsciously, 'I know she doesn't really love me, but if I go on acting as though she did, maybe I'll come to believe that she does.'

Where does this leave the experience of fragility and vulnerability? It leaves it as just that. We are fragile and vulnerable. Accepting that fact may help us to see what is really important, it may open our eyes to what is of real value, such as the enduring beauty of the natural world, and the importance of our relationships to others, in contrast to the superficial trappings of wealth and power. Those ramifications of the experience are as available to the atheist as to the theist. What the experience cannot by itself do is ground the belief in a transcendental realm of meaning, the belief in a divine power and purpose which can sustain us in our vulnerability by assuring us that good will prevail. The experience of vulnerability, and the experience of consolation for our vulnerability, are not the same. This is where I want to distinguish between the kinds of experience which are essential to our humanity, and the kinds of experience which it would be nice to have. Anyone can see the attraction of being able to believe that we are sustained by a higher power, and the attraction of being able to experience our fragility as a confirmation of that belief. But if the belief is to be warranted, there is no short-cutting the need for rational argument. The experience by itself is not enough.

Conclusion

I said at the beginning of this paper that I wanted to distinguish between experiences which it might be good to have and experiences which are an integral part of human life. I hope that my last case has helped to clarify the distinction. The experience of our vulnerability and dependence, and the awareness of what is really important which may be prompted by that experience, are deep features of human life. I suppose there are people who never, or only fleetingly, have that experience and that awareness, but a life without it would lack something. The feeling that, in our times of vulnerability, there is a higher power to sustain us, a guarantee of the resilience of goodness, is different. Atheists cannot have that feeling. They can recognise the attractions of being able to feel it, but it presupposes beliefs which an atheist cannot accept.

The same divergence is apparent in all the areas of experience which I have been surveying. In each of them there is a core experience which is an essential human experience and which is as available to the atheist as to the theist. There is also, in each case, an additional gloss which the theist can put on the experience, and which has its attractions. There is also, as we might expect, an overall pattern to the theistic extras. The theist who believes that there is a personal power which guarantees the resilience of goodness and which sustains us in our vulnerability is also likely to believe that that same personal power is at work in nature – that the transcendence of nature is not sheer otherness but reflects back at us in a higher form our human qualities of intelligence and emotion and will. The belief that that personal power, in nature and in our own lives, is working out some purpose, obscure to us but ultimately making for the triumph of good, provides the theist with a grand narrative, an overall story into which can be fitted the myriad of more particular stories which make sense of our lives. And the theist is also likely to believe that our responsiveness to beauty in art and nature, and our responsiveness to moral values, are intimations of the presence of that same transcendent but personal power.

Where the atheist, then, sees a number of essential but disparate forms of experience, the theist can see them as all manifestations of the same personal power at work in human lives, in human history and in the natural world. If, in each case, the theistic extra has its attractions, the very fact that they all fit into a single overall cohesive picture makes them all the more attractive.

What does the secular humanist have to offer instead? Only, I suppose, a kind of integrity – an insistence that though the prospect of an all-embracing cohesive belief-system is attractive, the attractiveness is not sufficient reason to endorse it. I do not of course suggest that theists necessarily lack integrity. I do not say that they adopt their religious beliefs solely because of the emotional appeal of such beliefs, I simply make the obvious point that the emotional appeal is not a good enough reason to adopt them, and that the secular humanist accepts this. The humanist will add that the various kinds of experience which I have been describing are in any case enough to sustain a full, rich and meaningful life. Humanism does not replace religious belief with some alternative grand narrative, some other synthesising doctrine, or some single supreme value which makes sense of everything. It says that we can live with plurality, with an untidy collection of diverse sources of strength and inspiration which, nevertheless, together are sufficient.[8]

[8]   I am grateful to members of the Philosophy departments at the University of Kent and at Queen's University Belfast for comments on earlier drafts, and to Sian Pettman for telling me what theism means to one theist.

7

DIVINE ACTION IN THE WORLD (SYNOPSIS)

Alvin Plantinga

The classical Christian idea of Providence is aptly summarised in a statement found in the Heidelberg Catechism:

> Providence is the almighty and ever-present power of God by which he upholds, as with his hand, heaven and earth and all creatures, and so rules them that leaf and blade, rain and drought, fruitful and lean years, food and drink, health and sickness, prosperity and poverty – all things, in fact, come to us not by chance but from his fatherly hand.[1]

Such a conception implies a *regularity* and *dependability* in the divinely created world. But traditional Christian belief also includes the idea of God's *special action* in the world – for example in the miracles described in the Old Testament (such as the parting of the Red Sea) and many of the events reported in the Gospels (such as Jesus's walking on water, his changing of water into wine, his miraculous healings, and his rising from the dead). Such miracles, moreover, are not supposed to have just occurred in Biblical times: according to classical Christian belief, God also now responds to prayers, for example by healings, and by working through the Holy Spirit in the hearts and minds of his children. In short, God constantly causes events in the world.

A belief in divine causal action in the world is thus standard Christian orthodoxy. But does it clash with any of the tenets of modern science? Many theologians seem to think that here there is indeed a 'science/religion problem'. Thus Rudolf Bultmann speaks of the historical method as including 'the presupposition that history is a unity in the sense of a closed continuum of effects in which individual events are connected by the succession of cause and effect.' And he goes on to assert that this continuum 'cannot be rent by the interference of supernatural, transcendent

---

[1]   Heidelberg Catechism, Question 27.

powers.'[2] In another passage, he goes so far as to say that 'It is impossible to use electric light and the wireless and to avail ourselves of modern medical and surgical discoveries, and at the same time to believe in the New Testament world of spirits and miracles.'[3] This general line is supported by John Macquarrie:

> The way of understanding miracles that appeals to breaks in the natural order and to supernatural intervention belongs to the mythological outlook and cannot commend itself in a post-mythological climate of thought . . . The traditional conception of miracle is irreconcilable with our modern understanding of both science and history. Science proceeds on the assumption that whatever events occur in the world can be accounted for in terms of other events that also belong within the world; and if on some occasions we are unable to give a complete account of some happening . . . the scientific conviction is that further research will bring to light further factors in the situation, but factors that will turn out to be just as immanent and this-worldly as those already known.[4]

In like manner, Langdon Gilkey observes that

> contemporary theology does not expect, nor does it speak of, wondrous divine events on the surface of natural and historical life. The causal nexus in space and time which the Enlightenment science and philosophy introduced into the Western mind . . . is also assumed by modern theologians and scholars; since they participate in the modern world of science both intellectually and existentially, they can scarcely do anything else. Now this assumption of a causal order among phenomenal events, and therefore of the authority of the scientific interpretation of observable events, makes a great difference to the validity one assigns to biblical narratives and so to the way one understands their meaning. Suddenly a vast panoply of divine deeds and events recorded in scripture are no longer regarded

---

[2]   Bultmann, Rudolf, *Existence and Faith: Shorter Writings of Rudolf Bultmann*, transl. S. M. Ogden, (New York: Meridian Books, 1960), pp. 291–2.
[3]   Bultmann, Rudolf. 'New Testament and Mythology', in *Kerygma and Myth: a Theological Debate*. ed. H. W. Bartsch, trans. R. H. Fuller (London: SPCK, 1957), p. 5.
[4]   Macquarrie, John, *Principles of Christian Theology* (New York: Scribner, 1966), pp. 226–7.

as having actually happened . . . Whatever the Hebrews believed, we believe that the biblical people lived in the same causal continuum of space and time in which we live, and so one in which no divine wonders transpired and no divine voices were heard.[5]

These various assertions of a 'religion/science problem' do not, however, succeed in making it clear what exactly the problem is supposed to be. According to the classical Christian and theistic picture of the world, God is a person, one who has knowledge, loves and hates, and aims or ends; he acts on the basis of his knowledge to achieve his ends. Second, God is all-powerful, all-knowing and wholly good. God has these properties essentially, and indeed necessarily: he has them in every possible world in which he exists, and he exists in every possible world. (Thus God is a necessarily existent concrete being, and the only necessarily existent concrete being.) Third, God has created the world. Fourth, as noted above in the quotation from the *Heidelberg Catechism*, God conserves, sustains, or maintains in being this world he has created. None of these claims of standard theistic belief appear in themselves to created a science/religion problem.

But there is a fifth claim, one that we are invited to see as problematic, namely that at least sometimes God acts in a way going beyond creation and conservation (for example in the case of miracles, but also in God's providential guiding of history, and his working in the hearts of people, and so on). Thus a divinely caused miracle would be a case of God's 'interfering', in Bultmann puts it – a violation of the 'hands-off theology' he advocates. Yet why should such 'interference' be somehow contrary to science? According to Philip Clayton, science has created a 'challenge to theology by its remarkable ability to explain and predict natural phenomena', and 'any theological system that ignores the picture of the world painted by scientific results is certain to be regarded with suspicion.' He goes on: 'In a purely deterministic universe there would be no room for God to work in the world except through the sort of miraculous intervention that Hume – and many of his readers – found to be so insupportable. Thus many, both inside and outside of theology, have abandoned any

---

[5]   'Cosmology, Ontology and the Travail of Biblical Language' in *The Journal of Religion* (July 1961) p. 185.

doctrine of divine action as incompatible with the natural sciences.'[6] Many scientists seem to share this view, for example H. Allen Orr, who in connection with miracles writes that 'no sensible scientist can tolerate such exceptionalism with respect to the laws of nature.'[7] So one might summarize the supposed problem as follows: science promulgates natural laws; if God did miracles or acted specially in the world, he would have to contravene these laws and miraculously intervene; and that's contrary to science.

The old scientific picture

Bultmann and those who follow him in thinking miracles are contrary to science are apparently thinking in terms of classical science (viz. Newtonian mechanics, and the later physics of electricity and magnetism represented by Maxwell's equations). According to the Newtonian world picture, God has created the world, which is like an enormous machine proceeding according to fixed laws – the laws of classical physics. Yet this is not sufficient for Anti-interventionism or Hands-off Theology; Newton himself (presumably) accepted the Newtonian World Picture, but he did not accept hands-off theology. Newton's laws describe how the world works *provided that the world is a closed (isolated)system*, subject to no outside causal influence. The great conservation laws deduced from Newton's laws are stated for *closed* or *isolated* systems. Thus, the principle of conservation of linear momentum states that 'where no resultant external force acts on a system, the total momentum of the system remains constant in magnitude and direction;' and the principle of conservation of energy states that 'the internal energy of an isolated system remains constant.'[8]

So these principles apply to closed or isolated systems. There is nothing here to prevent God from changing the velocity or direction of a particle, or from creating, *ex nihilo*, a full-grown horse. Energy is conserved in a closed system; but it is not part of

[6]   Clayton, Philip D., *God and Contemporary Science* (Edinburgh: Edinburgh University Press, 1997), p. 209.
[7]   *New York Review of Books*, May 13, 2004.
[8]   Sears and Zemanski, *University Physics* (Reading, MA: Addison-Wesley Publishing Co., 1964), pp. 186, 415.

Newtonian mechanics of classical science generally to declare that the material universe is indeed a closed system. (How could such a claim possibly be verified experimentally?)

To get hands-off theology, we need more than classical science as such. We would need, in addition, *determinism*, which is commonly defined as the thesis that the natural laws plus the state of the universe at any given time entail the state of the universe at any other time. Thus, Pierre Laplace states that 'we ought to regard the present state of the universe as the effect of its previous state, and as the cause of the one which is to follow. Given for one instant a mind which could comprehend all the forces by which nature is animated and the respective situation of the beings that compose it – a mind sufficiently vast to subject these data to analysis – it would embrace in the same formula the movements of the greatest bodies of the universe and those of the lightest atom; for it, nothing would be uncertain and the future, as the past, would be present to its eyes.'[9]

The idea, then, is that the material universe is a system of particles such that whatever happens at any time, together with the laws, determines whatever happens at any other time; i.e. the state of the universe at any time t together with the laws entails the state of the universe at any other time t^*. This deterministic picture is supposed to preclude special divine action (and also human freedom).

Several points about this should be noted. First, we need to ask: what are the laws like? If the laws are Humean descriptive generalizations (exceptionless regularities), determinism so conceived *does not* preclude either divine action or human action or even libertarian human freedom. On this Humean picture of natural laws, compatibilism would be perfectly correct: determinism is compatible with libertarian freedom. The same goes for David Lewis's conception of laws as supervening on particular matters of fact (being exceptionless regularities that display the best combination of strength and simplicity). Determinism is incompatible with human freedom only if the laws of nature are outside human control.

Second, Laplace is clearly thinking of the laws as the laws of classical science. The Laplacian picture is accurate only if the

---

[9]   Laplace, Pierre Simon, *A Philosophical Essay on Probabilities*, trans. F. W. Truscott (Mineola, NY: Dover Publications, 1995), p. 4.

universe is closed: only if God doesn't act specially in the world. If he did, that great Laplacian mind wouldn't be able to make those calculations. In other words, the Laplacian picture consists of the Newtonian picture *plus* the principle of closure – that the universe is a closed system. This is the picture guiding the thought of people like Bultmann, Macquarrie and Gilkey. An interesting point here is that in the name of being scientific and up to date they urge on us a picture of the world that is scientifically out of date by many decades. But in any case, classical science doesn't assert or include closure (or determinism). The laws describe how things go when the universe is causally closed, subject to no outside causal influence.

In this context, it is worth referring to J. L. Mackie's contrast between 'the order of nature' and 'a possible divine or supernatural intervention.' According to Mackie, 'the laws of nature describe the ways in which the world – including, of course, human beings – works when left to itself, when not interfered with. A miracle occurs when the world is not left to itself, when something distinct from the natural order as a whole intrudes into it.'[10] If we accept this, the natural laws would take the form:

(*NL*) When the universe is causally closed (God is not acting specially in the world), then *P*.

This seems a good description of the laws of nature and fits with the Newtonian picture. So thought of, the natural laws offer no threat to divine special action, including miracles. The Laplacian picture results only if we add that the universe is in fact a causally closed system and God never acts specially in it.

At this point someone might object: why can't we just as well say that the law is *P* itself, rather than *NL*? We could indeed say this; but then classical science as such doesn't imply that *P* is an exceptionless generalization; *P* holds just when nature is causally closed, and it is no part of classical science to assert that nature is causally closed. So again, there is no conflict with divine special action, including miracles.

In short, there is in classical science no objection to special divine action (or indeed to human free action, dualistically

---

[10]   Mackie, J. L., *The Miracle of Theism* (Oxford: Clarendon, 1982), pp. 19–20.

conceived). To get such an objection, we must add that the (material) universe is causally closed. But that is a metaphysical or theological add-on, not part of classical science. Classical science is perfectly consistent with special divine action including miracles (walking on water, rising from the dead, creating *ex nihilo* a full-grown horse). There is no religion/science conflict here; only a religion/metaphysics conflict.

So why do the theologians we have mentioned reject miracles and so on? The answer seems to be that they (mistakenly) think that miracles are contrary to science. A possible further objection they may have is that miracles would involve God's intervening in the world, which would involve his establishing regularities with one hand but undermining them with the other. But this is a theological objection, not one drawn from science. Nothing in classical science conflicts with miracles or special divine action.

The new scientific picture

The old Laplacian (and Newtonian) scientific picture has now been superseded by quantum mechanics. In particular, the laws of quantum mechanics are probabilistic rather than deterministic. Given a quantum mechanical system, for example a system of particles, these laws do not say which configuration will in fact result from the initial conditions, but instead they assign probabilities to the possible outcomes. Miracles (walking on water, rising from the dead, etc.) are clearly not incompatible with these laws. (They are no doubt very improbable; but we already knew that.) Further, on collapse interpretations, e.g., the collapse theories of Ghirardi, Rimini, and Weber, God could be the cause of the collapses, and of the way in which they occur. (One might perhaps think of this as a half-way house between occasionalism and secondary causation.) And on hidden variable interpretations, the laws describe how things go when God isn't acting specially. A further point to note is that if higher level laws supervene on (are determined by) lower level laws, nothing compatible with lower level laws will be incompatible with higher level laws.

Despite this, very many philosophers, theologians and scientists who are wholly aware of the quantum mechanics revolution still apparently find a problem with miracles and special divine action generally. A typical example may be found in 'The 'Divine Action Project',[11] a fifteen-year series of conferences and publications that began in 1988. So far these conferences have resulted in five or six books of essays involving some fifty or more authors from various fields of science together with philosophers and theologians, including many of the most prominent writers in the field: John Polkinghorne, Arthur Peacocke, Nancey Murphy, Philip Clayton and many others. This is certainly a serious and most impressive attempt to come to grips with the topic of divine action in the world. Nearly all of these authors believe that a satisfactory account of God's action in the world would have to be non-interventionistic. According to Wesley Wildman in his account of the Divine Action Project: '... The DAP project tried to be sensitive to issues of theological consistency. For example, the idea of God sustaining nature and its law-like regularities with one hand while miraculously intervening, abrogating or ignoring those regularities with the other hand struck most members as dangerously close to outright contradiction. Most participants certainly felt that God would not create an orderly world in which it was impossible for the creator to act without violating the created structures of order.'

According to Philip Clayton, the real problem here, apparently, is that it is very difficult to come up with an idea of divine action in the world in which such action would not constitute 'breaking natural law' or 'breaking physical law'. Arthur Peacocke comments as follows on a certain proposal for divine action, a proposal according to which God's special actions would be undetectable:

> God would have to be conceived of as actually manipulating micro-events (at the atomic, molecular, and according to some, quantum levels) in these initiating fluctuations on the natural world in order to produce the results at the macroscopic level which God wills. But such a conception of God's action . . . would then be no different in principle from that of God intervening in the order of nature, with all the problems that that evokes for a rationally coherent belief in God as the creator of that order.

---

[11]   So-called by Wesley Wildman, *Theology and Science* 2, p. 31ff.

But what, exactly, *is* the problem with intervention? More poignantly, what is intervention? We can say what it is on the old picture. As we saw, on the old picture the form of a natural law is

(*NL*) When the universe is causally closed (when God is not acting specially in the world), then *P*.

Let us now consider the result of deleting the antecedents from the laws, and call the conjunction of the *P*s 'L'. There is an intervention when an event E occurs such that there is an earlier state of the universe S such that S & L entails -E. But of course nothing like this account is available on the New Picture of science. So what would an intervention be? Four possible answers suggest themselves.

(1) The first suggestion is that an intervention occurs when God does something A that causes a state of affairs that would not have occurred if God had not done A. But on this account, any act of conservation would be an intervention; and presumably no one is worried about conservation.

(2) Alternatively, an intervention might be defined as what occurs when God performs an act A, which is neither conservation nor creation, that causes a state of affairs that would not have occurred if he had not performed A. But this appears to make intervention come down simply to God's acting specially in the world. Yet the original objection to special divine action was that it involves intervention. And in answer to the question 'What is intervention?' we are now told: 'Special divine action.' So apparently the problem with special divine action turns out to be special divine action.

(3) A third possibility is that one might define intervention as happening when God performs an act that is very improbable, given the previous states of the world. But in that case it is unclear what the problem is supposed to be. Why shouldn't God perform very improbable acts?

(4) Finally, one might define intervention in terms of the various low-level generalizations, not entailed by quantum mechanics, on which we normally rely: bread nourishes, people don't walk on water or rise from the dead, and so on. God would then be said to intervene when he causes an event contrary to one of those generalizations. But again, it is not clear what the problem with such interventions is supposed to be. Are we to suppose that the lower level regularities are like the laws of the

Medes and the Persians, so that once God has established one of them, not even he can act contrary to it? In any event, this kind of objection is philosophical or theological not scientific. There is nothing in science, under either the old or the new picture, that conflicts with, or even calls in to question, special divine action, including miracles.

INDEX

Note: page numbers in **bold** refer to chapters in this volume.

Adams, Robert   93, 95
aesthetics   95–9
afterlife, preparation for   21
agnosticism   2
   ineffability of God   63–70
   negative atheism   60
   Nicholas of Cusa   63–5
   truth-value of proposition   61
Akiva, Rabbi   5
St Anselm   61, 63
Aquinas, St Thomas
   argument from desire   54–7
   desire for God   41
   God not an entity   19
   Summa Theologiae   54
Aristotle
   akolasia   73–4
   becoming virtuous   38
   definition of soul   44
   virtue of humility   24–5
Arnold, Matthew   89
atheism
   awe of the natural world   30–1
   beauty and   95–9
   distinguished from theism   28–30
   experiences and   109–10
   experiences of theism   91–2
   explanations and imperatives   16
   inauthenticity of religious practice   13–14
   intention   14–16
   Jews   9
   meaningful narratives   99–102
   metaphysical belief   36–8
   moral authority and   92–5
   positive and negative   59–60
   religious practice and   1–3, 7
   transcendence and   102–5
   truth-value of proposition   60–1
   vulnerability and fragility   105–9
St Augustine of Hippo
   Confessions   57
   desire for God   41, 57
   natural religious orientation   52
authenticity
   heterodox orthopraxy and   13–14
awe
   secular/religious   30–5
Ayer, Sir Alfred   60

Bacon, Sir Francis   84
beauty
   atheist experience of   95–9
belief and faith
   being a believer   80–6
   British public polls   59
   certainty of   72–3
   experience and truth   107–8
   faith as commitment   87–8
   faith in the covenant   80–2
   metaphysical   36–8
   non-theistic practitioners   88–9
   orthopraxy and   2–3
   precariousness   82–3
   priority of practice   11–12
   rational   83–5
   secular humanist experience and   110
   test of   29

belief and faith (*cont'd*)
  in a whole narrative   85–6
Benatar, David
  'What's God Got to Do With It?
    Atheism and Religious
    Practice' **1–18**
Berry, G. G., paradox of   65
The Bible
  divine authorship   2
  glory   31
  love and reason   62
  meaningful narratives   99–100
  miracles and divine events
    111–13
  New Testament precedence
    3–4
blessings, thanksgiving   33–4
Bradlaugh, Charles   60
Braithwaite, Richard   89
Buddhism   82
  non-traditional Western   89
  parikalpita consciousness   78
  practitioners/believers   88–9
  samatha meditation   76
  transcendence   80, 89
Bultmann, Rudolf   111–12, 114

Christianity
  covenant with God   80–1
  life of the flesh/spirit   79–80
  miracles and divine events
    111
  moral wrongs   93
  Providence   111
  transcendence   103
  vary from Old Testament   3–4
Cicero, Marcus Tullius
  on the transcendent   51–2
Clayton, Philip   113, 118
Clough, Arthur Hugh
  'Hymnos Aumnos'   66–7
  'Qui Laborat Orat'   69–70
Confessions St Augustine   57
consciousness   78

Cottingham, John   105–7
  'What Difference Does It
    Make?' **19–38**
Crane, Stephen   75–6, 79
culture
  source of desires   48–50
Culture and Value (Wittgenstein)
  87
Cupitt, Don   89

De Docta Ignorantia (Nicholas of
  Cusa)   63–5
Dennett, Daniel
  evolutionary argument   52–3
Descartes, Rene   37–8
desire
  corresponding objects to
    48–50
  natural and artificial   48–50
  for transcendent fulfilment
    50–2
Dionysius the Areopagite   61
divine action
  and modern science   111–14
  in a Newtonian universe
    114–17
  in quantum universe   117–20
'Divine Action in the World'
  (Plantinga) **111–20**
The Divine Action Project   118
Donne, John   90
  Satyre III, Of Religion   74–5

Eliezer, Rabbi
  debate and miracles   5–6
Emblems Divine and Moral
  (Quarles)   39
emotions
  religious language   22–4
Epicurians
  virtues in a human world
    29
epistemology   42
  forms of knowledge   55–6

Eriugena, John Scotus
  Periphyseon 61–3
ethnicity 16
evil 94
evolution, purpose in 52–3
existence, human
  preparation for afterlife 21
existence of God 21–2
  argument from desire for 41
  John Scotus Eriugena on
    61–3
  Lewis and 47–8
  metaphysics and 36–8
  natural/supernatural effects
    40
  Peirce and the 'neglected
    argument' 43–6
  rational belief and 83–5
  St Anselm on 63

faith
  see belief and faith

Ghirardi, A. C. 117
Gilkey, Langdon 112–13
Glover, Jonathan 82–3
God
  as an entity 19–20
  covenant with 80–2
  defining 60
  divine action and 111–14
  glory of 30–5
  ineffability of 61, 63–70
  metaphors for/about 61–3
  metaphysical belief 36–8
  morality and 86
  as Other 52
  paradoxes of 64
  prayers to 66–9
  see also divine action; existence
    of God
God Still Matters (McCabe) 68
Graham, Gordon 94–5
Grahame, Kenneth
  The Wind in the Willows 32

Grayling, A. C. 72–3

Haldane, John
  aesthetics 95–7
  metanarrative 100
  'Philosophy, the Restless Heart
    and the Meaning of Theism'
    39–58
Haskala (Jewish enlightenment)
  2
Heidelberg Catechism 111
heresy
  forms of 2
  and religious practice 1–2
  hermeneutic framework 35
  heterodox orthopraxy 7–9
  explanations and imperatives
    16
  inauthenticity 13–14
  intention 14–16
Hillel I
  technicality vs spirit of law
    4
Hinduism 82
hope 35
  trust and 26–9
human beings
  prevalence of religion in 51
  significance of 29
  vulnerability and fragility
    105–9
Hume, David 113–14
  natural laws 115
humility 35
  awe and 31
  virtue of 24–6
'Hymnos Aumnos' (Clough)
  66–7

identity
  religious practice and 7–8
intention
  in religious practice 14–16
  three kinds of 15
Islamist beliefs 82

Jainism   82
Jesus Christ
    the afterlife and   21
    in art   97–9
    miracles of   111
    responsibility for death of   81
Job, Book of   26
Joshua, Rabbi   5–6, 12
Judaism
    covenant with God   80–1
    as ethnicity   10–11
    identity and   8–9
    Jewish enlightenment/
        Haskala   2
    law and   12–13
    moral wrongs   93
    orthodox heteropraxy   3–7
    practice over belief   11–12
    Reform   6
    Talmudic law   4–7
    Torah's mythology   12–13

Kant, Immanuel
    on awe   30–1
    conceivability   65
    explaining the aesthetic   45
    transcendence   76, 77
Kass, Leonard   33–4
Kenny, Anthony
    'Worshipping an Unknown
        God'   59–70
Kierkegaard, Søren   73
knowledge
    awareness of limits   63–4
    metaphors for God   60–2
Kureishi, Hanif   71, 73, 74–5, 90

language
    defining atheism   59–60
    expressing emotions of   22–4
    finding truth-value in   60
    humility   24–6
    religious language-games   66
    Scotus Eriugena on   61–3
Laplace, Pierre   115–16

law, religious
    evolution of   4–7
    Judaism and   12–13
    non-religious observance   7–8
law, secular   7
Lazarus, raising   21
Lewis, C. S.
    argument from desire   47–8,
        57
    desire for God   41
Lewis, David   115
'Lines Written above Tintern
    Abbey' (Wordsworth)   32–3
love
    and God's power   81

McCabe, Herbert
    God Still Matters   68
McGhee, Michael
    'Seeke True Religion, Oh,
        Where?'   71–90
Mackie, J. L.   116
Macquarrie, John   112
Maxwell, James Clerk   114
metanoia   28
metaphysics
    see philosophy
Michelangelo
    Creation of Adam   81
miracles
    see divine action
morality
    atheism and   110
    atheist experience of   92–5
    transcendence   78–9, 86–90
Moses
    crowns on God's letters   5
Motahari, Ayatollah Morteza   73
Murphy, Nancey   118

narratives   110
    meaningful   99–102
nature
    laws of   114–17
    secular/religious awe   30–5

transcendence and 103–5
Newton, Isaac 114–17
Nicholas of Cusa 61
De Docta Ignorantia 63–5
Norman, Richard
'The Varieties of Non-Religious
Experience' **91–110**

On Certainty (Wittgenstein) 85
Orr, H. Allen 114
orthodox heteropraxy 3–7

Pascal, Blaise 29, 107
awe of the universe 31
costs of belief 38
St Paul
perceiving God 51
trust and hope 26–7
Peacocke, Arthur 118
Peirce, C. S. 50
and Aquinas 57
argument from desire 51
desire for God 41
'Neglected Argument' 43–6
three Universes 43–4, 46
Phillips, D. Z. 42, 83
philosophy
argument over abstracts 39
belief in god 36–8
four positions on God 60–1
metaphysical heavy and light
20–1
wisdom and 42
'Philosophy, the Restless Heart
and the Meaning of Theism'
(Haldane) **39–58**
Piero della Francesca
The Resurrection 97–9
Plantinga, Alvin
'Divine Action in the World'
111–20
Plato
beyond the Cave 77
Polkinghorne, John 118

positivism
truth-value of proposition
60–1
prayer
to an ineffable God 66–9
thanksgiving in 33–4
The Prelude (Wordsworth) 103–5
Psalms, Book of
awe 31
on hope 27
on trust 26

Quarles, Francis
Emblems Divine and Moral 39
'Qui Laborat Orat' (Clough)
69–70
reason
non-contradiction and 64–5
religion
ethnicity and 10–11
evolutionary purpose of 52–3
framework of interpretation
24
the 'truly religious' 71–5
the untrained self 73–4
religious practice
atheism and 7
authenticity of 13–14
explanations and imperatives
16
heresy and 1–2
heterodox orthopraxy 7–9
intention 14–16
orthodox heteropraxy 3–7
precariousness 16–17
priority over belief 11–12
theology and 42
The Resurrection (Piero della
Francesca) 97–9
Rimini, A. 117
Russell, Bertrand
Berry's paradox 65
searching beyond 50–1

science
  miracles and 111–14
  Newtonian view 114–17
  quantum universe 117–20
Sea of Faith 89
secular humanism
  meaningful narrative 101–2
  see also agnosticism; atheism
'Seeke True Religion, Oh,
  Where?' (McGhee) **71–90**
Siddhartha 88–9
soul
  Aristotle's definition of 44
Stocker, Michael
  emotional states 23
Summa Theologiae (Aquinas) 54

Tennyson, Alfred, Lord 69
terrorism
  London bombings 82
thanksgiving 33–5
theism
  distinguished from atheism
    28–30
  philosophical position of 41–2
  religious/human experiences
    91–2, 109–10
  truth-value of proposition 61
transcendence 75–80, 110
  aesthetic 96–7
  atheist experience of 102–5
  moral 86–90
trust 26–8
truth
  in language 60
  making a leap of faith 107–8

Value and Virtue in a Godless
  Universe (Wielenberg) 27–8
'The Varieties of Non-Religious
  Experience' (Norman) **91–
  110**

virtue
  becoming/acting virtuous
    38
  Epicurean framework 29
  humility 24–6
  praxis of 35
  see also morality
Voltaire
  Lisbon earthquake 86
  seeking/finding truth 72–3,
    75
vulnerability, experience of
  105–9

Weber, A. 117
'What Difference Does It Make?
  The Nature and Significance
  of Theistic Belief'
  (Cottingham) **19–38**
'What's God Got to Do With It?
  Atheism and Religious
  Practice' (Benatar) **1–18**
Wielenberg, Erik
  Value and Virtue in a Godless
    Universe 27–8
Wildman, Wesley 118
Winch, Peter 81
The Wind in the Willows
  (Grahame) 32
wisdom 42
Wittgenstein, Ludwig 42
  On Certainty 85
  conceivability 65
  Culture and Value 87
Wordsworth, William
  'Lines Written above Tintern
    Abbey' 32–3
  The Prelude 103–5
  transcendence 77
'Worshipping an Unknown God'
  (Kenny) **59–70**
Wynn, Mark 23–4